Current
CONTROVERSIES

Human Trafficking

Other Books in the Current Controversies Series

Human Trafficking

Christina Fisanick, Book Editor

GREENHAVEN PRESS
A part of Gale, Cengage Learning

Detroit • New York • San Francisco • New Haven, Conn • Waterville, Maine • London

GALE
CENGAGE Learning

Christine Nasso, *Publisher*
Elizabeth Des Chenes, *Managing Editor*

© 2010 Greenhaven Press, a part of Gale, Cengage Learning

Gale and Greenhaven Press are registered trademarks used herein under license.

For more information, contact:
Greenhaven Press
27500 Drake Rd.
Farmington Hills, MI 48331-3535
Or you can visit our Internet site at gale.cengage.com

For product information and technology assistance, contact us at

Gale Customer Support, 1-800-877-4253
For permission to use material from this text or product, submit all requests online at www.cengage.com/permissions

Further permissions questions can be emailed to permissionrequest@cengage.com

Articles in Greenhaven Press anthologies are often edited for length to meet page requirements. In addition, original titles of these works are changed to clearly present the main thesis and to explicitly indicate the author's opinion. Every effort is made to ensure that Greenhaven Press accurately reflects the original intent of the authors. Every effort has been made to trace the owners of copyrighted material.

Cover image copyright © Wang Ying/Xinhua Press/Corbis.

LIBRARY OF CONGRESS CATALOGING-IN-PUBLICATION DATA

Human trafficking / Christina Fisanick, book editor.
    p. cm. -- (Current controversies)
    Includes bibliographical references and index.
    ISBN 978-0-7377-4142-1 (hardcover)
    ISBN 978-0-7377-4143-8 (pbk.)
    1. Human trafficking. 2. Human trafficking--Prevention--International cooperation. I. Fisanick, Christina.
    HQ281.H864 2009
    306.3'62--dc22
                                       2009028936

Printed in the United States of America
2 3 4 5 6   14 13 12 11 10

ED133

Contents

Chapter 1: Can Governments Reduce Human Trafficking?

Yes: Governments Can Reduce Human Trafficking

Chapter 2: What Can Individuals and Organizations Do to Reduce Human Trafficking?

Chapter 3: Can Global Cooperation Reduce Human Trafficking?

Chapter 4: What Role Do Victims Play in Human Trafficking?

Foreword

By definition, controversies are "discussions of questions in which opposing opinions clash" (Webster's Twentieth Century Dictionary Unabridged). Few would deny that controversies are a pervasive part of the human condition and exist on virtually every level of human enterprise. Controversies transpire between individuals and among groups, within nations and between nations. Controversies supply the grist necessary for progress by providing challenges and challengers to the status quo. They also create atmospheres where strife and warfare can flourish. A world without controversies would be a peaceful world; but it also would be, by and large, static and prosaic.

The Series' Purpose

The purpose of the Current Controversies series is to explore many of the social, political, and economic controversies dominating the national and international scenes today. Titles selected for inclusion in the series are highly focused and specific. For example, from the larger category of criminal justice, Current Controversies deals with specific topics such as police brutality, gun control, white collar crime, and others. The debates in Current Controversies also are presented in a useful, timeless fashion. Articles and book excerpts included in each title are selected if they contribute valuable, long-range ideas to the overall debate. And wherever possible, current information is enhanced with historical documents and other relevant materials. Thus, while individual titles are current in focus, every effort is made to ensure that they will not become quickly outdated. Books in the Current Controversies series will remain important resources for librarians, teachers, and students for many years.

In addition to keeping the titles focused and specific, great care is taken in the editorial format of each book in the series. Book introductions and chapter prefaces are offered to provide background material for readers. Chapters are organized around several key questions that are answered with diverse opinions representing all points on the political spectrum. Materials in each chapter include opinions in which authors clearly disagree as well as alternative opinions in which authors may agree on a broader issue but disagree on the possible solutions. In this way, the content of each volume in Current Controversies mirrors the mosaic of opinions encountered in society. Readers will quickly realize that there are many viable answers to these complex issues. By questioning each author's conclusions, students and casual readers can begin to develop the critical thinking skills so important to evaluating opinionated material.

Current Controversies is also ideal for controlled research. Each anthology in the series is composed of primary sources taken from a wide gamut of informational categories including periodicals, newspapers, books, U.S. and foreign government documents, and the publications of private and public organizations. Readers will find factual support for reports, debates, and research papers covering all areas of important issues. In addition, an annotated table of contents, an index, a book and periodical bibliography, and a list of organizations to contact are included in each book to expedite further research.

Perhaps more than ever before in history, people are confronted with diverse and contradictory information. During the Persian Gulf War, for example, the public was not only treated to minute-to-minute coverage of the war, it was also inundated with critiques of the coverage and countless analyses of the factors motivating U.S. involvement. Being able to sort through the plethora of opinions accompanying today's major issues, and to draw one's own conclusions, can be a complicated and frustrating struggle. It is the editors' hope that Current Controversies will help readers with this struggle.

Introduction

"Global human trafficking is big business."

The first movement intended to ban transatlantic human trafficking was led by William Wilberforce, whose bill to ban slavery was passed through the British parliament in 1833. Now, more than 150 years later, nearly all countries in the world have banned slavery. Despite these laws, many people remain enslaved. Statistics collected by the Polaris Project, one of the largest anti-trafficking organizations in the United States, estimate that in excess of eighteen thousand foreign nationals are trafficked annually in the United States. The estimated number of U.S. citizens who are sold into slavery each year is even higher. The forms of human trafficking have evolved since Wilberforce's time, but these statistics indicate that it remains a significant issue in the United States and elsewhere.

The United Nations' Protocol to Prevent, Suppress and Punish Trafficking in Persons, Especially Women and Children defines human trafficking as "the recruitment, transportation, transfer, harboring or receipt of persons, by means of the threat or use of force or other forms of coercion, of abduction, of fraud, of deception, of the abuse of power or of a position of vulnerability or of the giving or receiving of payments or benefits to achieve the consent of a person having control over another person, for the purpose of exploitation." The June 2007 "Trafficking in Persons Report," published by the U.S. government, succinctly defines human trafficking by noting, "The common denominator of trafficking scenarios is the use of force, fraud, or coercion to exploit a person for profit. A victim can be subjected to labor exploitation, sexual exploitation, or both."

Global human trafficking in its various forms is big business. The International Labor Organization estimates profits from human trafficking at $44.3 billion per year, with the largest share coming from the sex trade. According to the 2009 United Nations "Global Report on Trafficking in Persons," 79 percent of persons trafficked are done so for sexual purposes. Children as young as infants are sold into sexual slavery, as is revealed in the award-winning documentary, *Born into Brothels.*

However, the sale of persons into sexual bondage is not an international phenomenon alone. According to a three-part series that aired on *The Early Show*, "Human trafficking is a low-risk, high-profit enterprise, and because it looks to the casual observer—and even to cops—like garden-variety prostitution, it is tolerated." Producers of the series *Against Their Will* conducted interviews and collected data about hundreds of American teenagers who were bought and sold in U.S. prostitution rings. They often are drugged and forced into sexual encounters with strangers while their captors collect the money. It can take many years, according to the series, for these young people to completely reveal what has happened to them for fear of retaliation from their pimps.

Sexual slavery is not the only form that modern human trafficking takes. Elizabeth Pathy Salett, of the National Multicultural Institute, states, "Globalization and the promise of good jobs and economic opportunity serve to lure women and men to what they believe will bring them a better life." Unfortunately, these persons often are forced to work under severe conditions for little or no pay. An investigative report published in 2003 in the *Palm Beach Post* revealed the working conditions of migrant farm workers in Florida. According to Christine Evans and her coauthors, "Florida farmworkers live in some of the worst housing in the country. Aging, rat-infested trailers dot the state, owned by slumlords and rented by crew leaders eager to make a buck off poor migrants."

In other situations, workers are forced to toil under difficult conditions to pay off debts accrued by themselves or family members. Often these debts are manufactured by company owners eager to make a profit from cheap labor. Although indentured servitude is most commonly associated with colonial America, in which immigrants paid for their passage to the new world by working for their patrons for a set number of years, modern debt slavery still exists. In fact, the International Labor Organization estimates that 12.3 million people are enslaved by debt bondage at any given time. In many instances this kind of slavery never ends, because the debts are impossible to repay. According to data collected by the Stop Violence Against Women (SVAW) project advanced by the United Nations Development Fund for Women (UNIFEM), "In situations of debt bondage, women become virtual prisoners, as they are unable to ever earn back the amount purportedly owed to the traffickers." Further, SVAW adds, "Trafficked women are prevented from escaping their situation through debt bondage as well as retention of travel documents, violence and threats of violence against themselves or their families."

In the foreword to "Freedom Denied: Forced Labor in California," a study conducted by the Human Rights Center at the University of California at Berkeley, the authors note, "A century and a half after the Emancipation Proclamation, Americans should not have to be dealing with forced labor. But the responsibility of doing so rests on all of us.... There are thousands of people laboring within our borders in shocking conditions, usually hidden from sight." The authors of the viewpoints in *Current Controversies: Human Trafficking* debate ways of combating human trafficking in all its forms in the following chapters: Can Governments Reduce Human Trafficking? What Can Individuals and Organizations Do to Reduce Human Trafficking? Can Global Cooperation Reduce Human Trafficking? and What Role Do Victims Play in Human Trafficking? In the end, ensuring that humans are free from future enforced bondage would be a worthy legacy for any generation.

Can Governments Reduce Human Trafficking?

Chapter Preface

World governments have been striving for decades to reduce human trafficking taking place as a result of the sex trade. In 2003, then–U.S. president George W. Bush signed into law the antiprostitution pledge in an effort to encourage international organizations to help eliminate sex work around the world. The pledge requires nongovernmental organizations (NGOs) that receive federal funding for HIV/AIDS or for human trafficking prevention to implement policies opposing prostitution and sex trafficking. The original pledge applied only to international organizations, but it has since expanded to cover domestic groups as well. Although many governments and organizations have been supportive of the pledge, several others have responded to it unfavorably.

The implementation of the antiprostitution pledge marked a crucial step in the U.S. government's war against human trafficking. Specifically, it takes aim at the connection between the sale of women and girls for sex and the sale of humans internationally. In addition, its passage demonstrates the U.S. government's stance on the relationship between HIV/AIDS and the sex trade. In a 2007 statement supporting the pledge, Christian Medical Association (CMA) CEO David Stevens wrote, "We know from the research that prostitution spreads AIDS and accounts for much of human trafficking worldwide." Like the CMA, other organizations assert that the pledge is a step forward in the battle against these two serious human conditions.

On the other hand, opponents have argued that the pledge works against the prevention of HIV/AIDS and human trafficking by excluding the group most valuable in the fight: sex workers. In a 2005 letter to the U.S. director of foreign assistance, several international organizations, including Save the Children and CARE, expressed their opposition to the pledge.

In defense of the letter, Maurice I. Middleburg, then–acting president of EngenderHealth, a sixty-two-year-old public health charity working in sixteen countries, told the *Washington Post* that the pledge "risks further stigmatizing a population [prostitutes] that is already very difficult to reach." Later that year, Brazil turned down millions of dollars in HIV/AIDS prevention funds because of the government pledge. Pedro Chequer, the country's national AIDS director reported to the U.S. magazine the *Nation* that "sex workers are part of implementing our AIDS policy and deciding how to promote it. They are our partners. How could we ask prostitutes to take a position against themselves?"

Nonetheless, the U.S. Department of Justice continues to take a strong stance against prostitution, arguing in a 2005 report that "the abolition of prostitution, the driving force behind sex trafficking, is integral to the abolition of human trafficking." Clearly, few organizations would argue that sexual slavery or any other kind of forced sexual activity should be condoned, but some groups have noted the importance of including sex workers in the conversation. As the authors in this chapter argue, governments can often reduce human trafficking by enacting and enforcing policies. It remains to be seen whether the U.S. antiprostitution pledge can do just that.

Laws and More Education Can Stop Child Trafficking

Debbie Ariyo

Debbie Ariyo is founder and executive director of Africans Unite Against Child Abuse (AFRUCA), which promotes the welfare of African children living in the United Kingdom.

The two brothers walked through our office doors at Afruca—Africans Unite Against Child Abuse. Sobbing, they recounted details of their terrible experiences spanning many years at the hands of various relatives to whom they were sent as children for a "better life" by their mother following the death of their father in Nigeria. They ended up as domestic slaves.

Now in their mid-twenties, the two young men have spent the bulk of their lives in the UK [United Kingdom] in abject penury. Denied the opportunity of a decent education, they are now homeless, jobless and unable to produce any documentation as proof of their identities. Effectively, they are in limbo, living from hand to mouth, not sure of their next meal or their next bed for the night. These two young men are part of a growing underclass of young people trafficked into the UK as child slaves. . . .

As a result of a media campaign run by Afruca on African satellite TV stations, we have continued to receive young people who have tales of woe similar to the two brothers. We have supported at least 15 young people in various ways since January 2007 to enable them [to] deal with the impact of trafficking and exploitation so they can move on with their lives. While all their stories are different, their experiences of abuse and exploitation as domestic slaves are very similar. More and more young people are coming to us for help, evidence of the growing phenomenon of child domestic slavery in this country.

Our experience is supported by recent research into child trafficking. A recent report produced by the Child Exploitation and Online Protection Centre (CEOP) identified 330 victims of trafficking, a third of them coming from different African countries with most of them destined for domestic slavery. This is corroborated by the results of another study on child trafficking in the north of England by ECPAT UK [End Child Prostitution and Trafficking].

Is Exploitation a Nigerian Problem?

Without wishing to stigmatise any community, it is pertinent to add that all the 15 victims mentioned above, including the two brothers, are of Nigerian origin. In the same vein, all the victims of domestic slavery identified in the two research reports referred to above are also all from Nigeria. As a Nigerian myself, this fact is quite disconcerting. Why are Nigerian children being trafficked into the UK for domestic slavery?

Instead of the better life and the good education promised, only a childhood of exploitation awaits.

The practice of using children for domestic servitude is undoubtedly a very common phenomenon in Nigeria itself. According to local non-governmental organisations campaigning against this practice, almost every middle class household employs domestic servants many of whom are children. Due to the growing poverty level, the widening gap between rich and poor Nigerians, many parents are wont to give their children to better off relatives in the belief that they will be well looked after and given an opportunity of either going to school or learning a vocation. However, most of these children end up being used as slaves and servants.

Yet the idea of giving children away to relatives is nothing new or strange in many African countries. The practice of fostering, where children are given to relatives to look after is not an act borne out of cruelty or ignorance. In the past, this system has afforded many children from poor backgrounds the opportunity of a good education leading to a prosperous future. The notion that it takes a village to raise a child meant that the extended family were responsible for ensuring children had access to a decent life which their poor parents were unable to give them. Unfortunately, this system of community support has been abused by unscrupulous individuals with ulterior motives. The sad case of Victoria Climbié, the Ivorien girl trafficked into the UK and tortured to death by her relative comes to mind here.

The estimated two million Nigerians here are probably the most rooted nationals from any African country in the UK, bearing in mind that many have been living in or visiting the country since the 1960s and 1970s. With a growing middle class population, it is not surprising that the practice of fostering is equally taking hold here as well. Unfortunately, however, many children and their parents have been deceived into coming to the UK for a so-called better life and a good education. Instead, these children end up being used as slaves, to look after the families of their exploiters and cater for their every need. Many have been subjected to a life of suffering, multiple abuse, excessive child labour and harm. Instead of the better life and the good education promised, only a childhood of exploitation awaits.

The physical abuse experienced in many cases result in long-term poor health. Some of the victims we worked with at Afruca were also sexually abused by their exploiters. Most terrible of all is the rupture with their own families. A young girl we supported was brought into the UK at the age of nine years. Now at the age of 19 she has never been in touch with any member of her immediate family as she was prevented from doing so by her exploiters. It is doubtful whether she will ever be able to locate them.

Denial of the Right to Family Life

This broken family link, the denial of rights to a decent family life, is a serious form of emotional abuse. Added to the lack of parental care given by the exploiters, many child victims exist in an emotional vacuum, with no love, no affection, and no attention ever paid to them. The deceit, abuse and exploitation experienced at the hands of those they expected to care for them and help them achieve a better life result in a deep emotional and psychological scarring. In fact, many of the victims who come to us have revealed that at one time or another, they either attempted suicide or had many suicidal thoughts.

Yet the implications of their experiences do not end with their slavery. Every single young person we have been in contact with has a serious problem proving their true identity. In many instances, traffickers employ false identities in order to be able to procure travel documents to bring their child victims into the country. Now as adults, many of them have no way of ascertaining their true names, age and date of birth because authentic documentation is unobtainable.

Until someone is prosecuted, this practice will continue unabated.

One consequence is that young people are disbelieved by the authorities when they attempt to regularise their status in the UK and they cannot get jobs. Many victims of trafficking do come to the attention of different agencies—be it social services, schools, doctors and others. But practitioners are often unable to identify the indicators of abuse and exploitation and to safeguard the young people. At least one victim we worked with had run away to seek help and support from her local social services department. Unfortunately, not only was she denied any form of help, she was reprimanded for running away from home and was returned to her exploiters.

No Prosecutions of Exploiters

No one has ever been prosecuted here for child domestic slavery. Many of the victims we have worked with have taken the steps to report their cases although to date no action has been taken. Yet the UK government is a signatory to the European Convention on Human Rights, articles 3 and 4 of which clearly highlight the rights of people not to be subjected to torture or to inhuman or degrading treatment or to be held in slavery or servitude. Since the government is obliged to protect these rights, it is a mystery that no one has ever been prosecuted.

Until someone is prosecuted, this practice will continue unabated. The government has got a policy in the form of its National Action Plan on Human Trafficking, but it is not enough. Not only should their exploiters be made to face the music, but victims need to be given the support and assistance they require to enable them to prosecute their exploiters and seek compensation for their lost childhoods.

It is also imperative that action is taken to raise awareness in source countries such as Nigeria about the implications of handing children over to a "better life". Unless everyone is aware of the facts, the endless stream of children looking for a better life will continue unabated.

Legalizing Prostitution Increases Human Trafficking

Richard Poulin

Richard Poulin is a professor of sociology at the University of Montreal in Canada. His research and teaching focuses on pornography and other social issues.

Several countries have legalized prostitution since the start of the new millennium. . . .

In my book, *La Mondialisation Des Industries du Sexe* [*The Globalization of Sex Industries*], I show that violence is intrinsically interwoven with prostitution, that it is an essential element of it. While the conditions under which prostitution is carried out can undoubtedly exacerbate its inherent violence, it is primarily the social relationships which underpin prostitution that are the fundamental cause of this violence. The pimps' recruiting methods are not really the simple accumulation of private "abusive" behaviours, but occur within a structured system which requires violence. The violence committed by a substantial number of customers derives from the fact that the mercenary nature of the transaction confers upon them a position of domination.

Prostitution Violence Is Inherent

Prostitution is ontologically a form of violence. It feeds on violence and in turn amplifies it. Abduction, rape, submission—there are submission camps in a number of European countries, not only in the Balkans and in Central Europe, but also in Italy, where submission is called "schooling"—terror and murder are still the midwives and outriders of this industry; they are essentially not only for market development, but

Richard Poulin, "The Legalization of Prostitution and Its Impact on Trafficking in Women and Children," Sisyphe.org, February 26, 2005. Copyright © Sisyphe 2002–2007. Reproduced by permission.

also for the "manufacture" of the "goods" as they contribute to making prostituted people "functional"—this industry demands total availability of the body. A study of street prostituted people in England established that 87% of them had been victims of violence during the past 12 months; 43% were suffering the consequences of serious physical abuse. A research study in Chicago showed that 21.4% of women working as escorts and exotic dancers had been raped more than 10 times. An American study in Minneapolis showed that 78% of prostituted people had been victims of rape by pimps and customers, on average, 49 times a year. 49% had been the victims of abduction and had been transported from one state to another and 27% had been mutilated. I could multiply the data generated by field studies.

Every year, approximately 500,000 women who are victims of trafficking are released onto the prostitution market in the countries of Eastern Europe.

What I want to emphasize here is that the women and children who are the objects of trafficking for the purpose of prostitution as well as the vast majority of prostituted people, have very often been subjected to violence. A large number of them are supplied to the market on a "turnkey" basis: "Any woman can be broken in 10 days and turned into a prostitute", in the words of the Bulgarian manager of a rehabilitation centre. Their abduction by traffickers of all kinds, who become their owners, their "commodification"—human beings metamorphosed into "goods" that are sold on the sex market, their depersonalization, and then their consumption demand the rape of their humanity and require violence. The violence to which prostituted people are subjected is multiple and often unspeakable, indescribable. Violence is intrinsic to prostitution: the commodification and merchandising are aimed at forcing the sexes to submit to the satisfaction of the sexual pleasure of others. The second is also inherent: a person becomes prostituted as a result of sexual, physical, psychic (in 90% of cases, according to a range of studies), social and economic violence. The third is linked to the expansion of prostitution and to the ensuing deterioration of the conditions to which prostituted people are subjected: "The customer has no further hesitation about being increasingly violent towards the prostitute and today she must be extremely vigilant", claims Chant, of the Bus des Femmes, an association established in Paris over a decade ago by former prostituted people.

The conditions under which prostitution is exercised are thus not the cause of this violence, although this is the thrust of the organizations that argue in favour of the total decriminalization of prostitution or of its legalization. The cause is to be found not in the conditions under which prostitution is carried out, but in the carrying out of it.

The Scale of the Sex Industries

Every year, approximately 500,000 women who are victims of trafficking are released onto the prostitution market in the countries of Eastern Europe; 75% of the women who are victims of this trafficking are 25 years of age or under, and an indeterminate, but very large, percentage of them are minors. Some 4 million women and children annually are the victims of the worldwide trafficking for the purpose of prostitution. In 2001, it was estimated that the number of prostituted people in the world was 40 million, a figure that continues to rise. The phenomenon assumes unimaginable proportions in some countries, accounting for between 0.25% and 1.5% of the population in the Philippines, Malaysia, Taiwan, etc.

The prostitution industry accounts for 5% of the GDP [gross domestic product] of the Netherlands, between 1 and 3% of Japanese GDP and in 1998, the International Labour Organization (ILO) estimated that prostitution accounted for between 2 and 14% of the total economic activity in Thailand, Indonesia, Malaysia and the Philippines....

The regulation (legalization) of prostitution has thus not improved the fate of prostituted people.

The example of the Netherlands provides a good indicator of the expansion of the sex industry in recent decades and the growth of trafficking for the purpose of prostitution: 2,500 prostituted people in 1981, 10,000 in 1985, 20,000 in 1989 and 30,000 in 1997. The Netherlands has become a preferred destination in the world of sex tourism. In Amsterdam, where there are 250 brothels, 80% of the prostituted people are of foreign origin and "70% of them have no papers", as they are victims of trafficking. In 1960, 95% of prostitutes in the Netherlands were Dutch, whereas by 1999 the figure was a mere 20%. In Denmark, where prostitution is also legal, the number of prostituted people of foreign origin who are victims of trafficking has increased ten-fold over the past decade. In Austria, 90% of prostituted people are originally from other countries. In 2003, the number of victims of trafficking for the purpose of prostitution was estimated at 20,000 annually, compared to 2,100 annually at the start of the previous decade. In the ten years from 1990 to 2000, 77,500 young foreign women have fallen prey to traffickers. These young women, who are frequently minors, and who can be purchased on the markets in the Balkans for US $600, are subjected to an average of between 30 and 100 sexual contacts a day. Ten years ago, the number of prostituted people of Greek origin was estimated at 3,400; this figure remains more or less the same today, but with the explosion of the prostitution industry, the number of prostituted people of foreign origin has multiplied by ten. The revenues derived from prostitution in Greece are estimated at US $7.5 billion a year.

Legalization Benefits the Wrong People

Talking of foreign prostituted people means trafficking in human beings for the purpose of prostitution (and the production of pornography), which obviously implies that the trafficking is organized. Organized pimping, which is controlled by organized crime, is the major supplier of the night clubs and brothels, of which there are 700 in the Netherlands, where prostitution has been regulated since October 1, 2000. This legalization, which was intended to benefit prostituted people, according to its advocates, is probably a failure, since only 4% of them have registered. This legalization was supposed to put an end to prostitution of minors. However, the Organization for the Rights of the Child, the headquarters of which is in Amsterdam, estimates that the number of minors who are prostituted in the Netherlands has increased from 4,000 in 1996 to 15,000 in 2001, including at least 5,000 who are of foreign origin. In Vienna, Austria, the number of prostituted people was estimated at the start of 2000 at between 6,000 and 8,000; only 600 of them were registered. Ten years later, there were 800 registered prostituted people and approximately 2,800 illegal prostituted people. In 1995, the number of registered prostituted people had dropped to 670, whereas the number of illegals had climbed to 4,300.

As the experience in the Netherlands, Greece and Austria shows, the number of "legal" prostituted people, those who are natives of the country, is gradually dropping (in relative or absolute terms) and the number of prostituted people who are clandestine, illegal, who have a tourist visa or who are victims of trafficking is increasing. The regulation (legalization) of prostitution has thus not improved the fate of prostituted people, in contrast to the claims of activists who are in favour of such a policy. But legalization does represent a goldmine for the pimps, whose activity is now legal: over the past 10 years, the activities of the sex industry in the Netherlands have increased by 25%. Thanks to its liberal legislation, the Dutch government takes in US $1.202 billion annually in taxes, thereby becoming one of Europe's largest pimps. . . .

Government policies are . . . a decisive factor in the proliferation of prostitution industries and its corollary, trafficking.

The Expansion of Global Prostitution

The promoters of the legalization of prostitution in Australia maintained that such a step would solve such problems as the control by organized crime of the sex industry, the deregulated expansion of that industry and the violence to which street prostituted people are subjected. In fact, the legislation has solved none of these problems: on the contrary, it has given rise to new ones, including child prostitution, which has increased significantly since legalization. Brothels are expanding and the number of illegal brothels exceeds the number of legal ones. Although there was a belief that legalization would make possible control of the sex industry, the illegal industry is now "out of control". Police in Victoria estimate that there are 400 illegal brothels as against 100 legal ones. Trafficking in women and children from other countries has increased significantly. The legalization of prostitution in some parts of Australia has thus resulted in a net growth of the industry. One of the results has been the trafficking in women and children to "supply" legal and illegal brothels. The "sex entrepreneurs" have difficulty recruiting women locally to supply an expanding industry, and women from trafficking are more vulnerable and more profitable. The traffickers sell such women to the owners of Victoria's brothels for US $15,000 each. They are held in servitude by this debt. The weekly profits derived from the trafficking in women in Australia by the prostitution industry is estimated at $1 million. . . .

The legalization of prostitution thus generates a colossal expansion of this industry and of the trafficking which is its corollary.

An "abolitionist" country like France, with a population estimated at 61 million, has half as many prostituted people on its territory as does a small country like the Netherlands (16 million) and 20 times fewer than a country like Germany, with a population of around 82.4 million. In Sweden, where legislation has been passed to prosecute the customers and to decriminalize the activities of prostituted people, it is estimated that there are only about 100 prostituted people in the country for around 9 million inhabitants. In the capital, Stockholm, the number of street prostitutes has dropped by two-thirds and the number of customers has dropped by 80%. In addition, [according to French correspondent Axel Gyldén,] "Sweden is the only country in Western Europe not to have been submerged by the tidal wave of girls from Eastern Europe following the fall of the Berlin wall". In neighbouring Finland, it is estimated that 15,000 to 17,000 people become victims of trafficking for the purpose of prostitution annually.

The most recent research, carried out by London Metropolitan University, at the request of the Scottish government and published in 2004 on its government website, "confirms what several prior studies have shown, namely that the 'sex industries', sexual tourism, child prostitution and violence against prostituted people have increased markedly in all the countries that have liberalized their prostitution laws and turned pimps into respectable businessmen."

Government policies are accordingly a decisive factor in the proliferation of prostitution industries and its corollary, trafficking.

Policies favourable to the legalization of prostitution and trafficking for the purpose of prostitution form part of an international offensive, mounted by the countries that advocate regulation, against the abolitionist Convention adopted by the

UN in 1949, the Convention for the Suppression of Human Trafficking and the Exploitation of the Prostitution of Others. These countries have introduced in international or regional conferences (especially in Europe) the concepts of "forced prostitution" and "forced trafficking" in contrast to "voluntary prostitution" and "voluntary or consenting trafficking"....

The Industrialization of Prostitution

Humankind is witnessing the industrialization of prostitution, trafficking in women and children, pornography and sex tourism. The various sectors of the sex industry are flourishing; they are organized and managed by networks of pimps and organized crime. The liberalization of the laws governing prostitution in some countries has allowed the pimps involved in organized crime to acquire, emerging from the underground, the status of entrepreneurs and respected business partners. The criminal markets are naturally integrated into the legal markets where they are able to launder money with complete impunity. They now play a major role in the world economy. The United Nations Development Program (UNDP) estimates that gross criminal product makes up 15% of world trade. The sex markets account for a sizeable share of this. It is estimated that the profits from trafficking women for the purpose of prostitution alone now generate more money than trafficking in firearms or drugs. The sex trade industry [is] increasingly regarded as an entertainment industry and prostitution as "legitimate work".

There are two major consequences of the legalization of prostitution. First, the institutional officialization (legalization) of sex markets strengthens the activities of organized pimping and organized crime. Secondly, such strengthening, accompanied by a significant increase in prostitution-related activities and in trafficking, brings with it a deterioration not only in the general condition of women and children, but also, in particular, that of prostituted people and the victims of trafficking for the purpose of prostitution.

While the total decriminalization of prostitution—equivalent of the law of the jungle—is not regarded favourably by any country, the legalization of prostitution brings with it a number of problems that I have examined. The alternative is the policy adopted by Sweden, which criminalizes those who benefit from prostitution—the pimps and the customers—and decriminalizes the activities of the prostituted people, who are regarded as the prey and the victims of organized pimping.

The Trafficking Victims Protection Reauthorization Act Has Been Effective

Deborah Pryce

Deborah Pryce is a former Republican member of the U.S. House of Representatives for Ohio's Fifteenth Congressional District and the former chair of the House Republican Conference.

After weeks of controversy and amid strong opposition in Congress, Dubai Ports World (DPW), a company owned by the government of Dubai, an emirate of the United Arab Emirates (UAE), abandoned its plans to manage six ports on the East Coast of the United States. Our ports have long presented a security vulnerability, and Congress and the American people were rightfully concerned about the propriety of allowing a company owned by a foreign government to manage our nation's seaports.

During the course of Congress' investigation into the process by which DPW was granted the contract, as Congress examined the UAE and its relationship to the U.S., an issue of concern came to light: the UAE's troubling record on human rights. The UAE is home to a disturbing human trafficking trend, the selling of young boys into the UAE's lucrative camel-racing industry to be unpaid jockeys. In other words: slavery.

Slavery is supposed to be a distant memory, but in truth, it's alive and well—and the use of these unpaid camel jockeys is just one example of it. The State Department's Trafficking in Persons Office estimates that up to 800,000 people are annually trafficked across international borders, human beings bought and sold for $10 billion every year.

Approximately 80% of them are women, and as many as half of them are children. Human trafficking is one of the most profitable businesses for international organized crime, following only drugs and weapons, and is one of the fastest-growing criminal activities in the world.

Here at home the numbers are more modest, but our outrage is not. Approximately 18,000 women and children from around the world are brought into this country each year, some smuggled illegally, others lured with visas and the promise of jobs and then coerced into slavery upon arrival. And this does not include the number of persons trafficked from within the United States. The city of Toledo, Ohio, was recently identified as a center of teenage prostitution and sex slavery. Ohio newspapers were full of stories of the girls trapped in this ring, girls as young as 12 or 13, raped, beaten, abused, their bodies sold to enrich their captors. Prosecutors indicted 31 men and women in the Toledo area on charges of taking minors across state lines as sex slaves.

Our Moral Obligation

We have a moral obligation to fight this evil. Trafficking in human beings is an assault on our most cherished beliefs, that every human being has freedom and dignity and worth. A nation that stands for the freedom and dignity of every human being cannot tolerate the exploitation of the innocent on its own soil. This needs to be a national priority, because it is a global outrage.

[In its first two years, Operation Innocence Lost] rescued more than 200 child victims and helped uncover the Toledo sex trafficking ring.

In 2005, I led a congressional delegation to Italy, Greece, Albania and Moldova to meet with trafficking victims and government officials and discuss ways to end this crime and protect its victims. During this trip, and later during hearings I held as chairman of a House financial services subcommittee, I heard testimony on the economic and financial implications of human trafficking, as well as the heartrending stories of trafficking victims. Their stories of rape, torture and routine brutality are simply beyond description.

[In 2006] Congress passed, and President [George W.] Bush signed, the Trafficking Victims Protection Reauthorization Act. This legislation strengthens the original Trafficking Victims Protection Act to keep the U.S. at the forefront of the global war on this modern-day slavery. Included in the $360-million package is an expansion of the Operation Innocence Lost program, a nationwide initiative that aggressively pursues sex traffickers and child prostitution rings. [In its first two years,] the program rescued more than 200 child victims and helped uncover the Toledo sex trafficking ring.

Congress has also recently taken steps to target demand for sex trafficking. Provisions of the Trafficking Victims Protection Act that I authored along with [Representative] Carolyn Maloney (D.-N.Y.) will provide state and local law enforcement with new tools to target demand and investigate and prosecute sex trafficking, fund a national conference on best practices for reducing demand for sex trafficking and fund a review of the incidence of sex trafficking in the U.S., to provide us with a more accurate picture of the scope of this problem.

Our law enforcement strategy must be wedded to a vigorous partnership between government agencies and private and religious organizations on the front lines of this struggle. For years these groups have helped rescue and support trafficking victims and raise awareness about the fight against human trafficking.

Human trafficking is a heinous crime, a betrayal of one of the most basic obligations of morality—the obligation to defend the innocent. The presence of this scourge in our midst cannot and will not be tolerated. But those who would so debase themselves and the human family by buying and selling women and children are beyond mere reproach. They will not respond to outrage, but to action.

Laws Meant to Deter Illegal Aliens Adversely Affect Trafficking Victims

Mary Ellen Dougherty and Jane Burke

Mary Ellen Dougherty is the coordinator of education and out-reach for the U.S. Conference of Catholic Bishops' program against human trafficking. Jane Burke is a facilitator and consultant for the conference and the former national manager of the Justice for Immigrants program.

Undocumented immigrants victimized by human traffick-ers are among the most vulnerable of the people affected by U.S. immigration policy. Many of them embark on their journey as hopeful migrants but run up against limits on legal migration and jobs. For the promise of honest work and earn-ings to share with their families back home, they are willing to risk the unknown to enter this country and stay here. More desperate than dream-ridden, many such migrants have ended up as victims of human trafficking.

The Realities of Modern Slavery

By definition, a victim of human trafficking is one who has been forced, through fraud or other coercive means, into la-bor or sexual exploitation for commercial purposes. Their la-bor can take the form of debt bondage, peonage or any work under slave-like conditions. Victims have been forced to work in brothels, factories, farms or even private homes without freedom of movement or adequate wages. Most of them typi-cally work under harsh conditions as well. Seduced or misled by false promises, the victims are often held in place by psychological or physical force or both. Some are coerced by threats to their loved ones in their home country. Such migrants are also captives, unable to move on without great risk.

Once victims of human trafficking are identified as such by U.S. authorities, they become eligible for such government benefits as legal aid, medical care and education, the same benefits available to refugees. But the one benefit they want most, the right to work, is not given them.

Over the course of 20 months [in 2007 and 2008], the U.S. Conference of Catholic Bishops [U.S.C.C.B.] has facilitated services in the United States for 569 foreign nationals from 69 countries as victims of human trafficking. Of these, 57 percent were victims of exploitation in the workplace, 32 percent were victims of sexual exploitation and 11 percent were victims of both kinds of human trafficking. Although some of the foreign nationals were in the U.S. legally, most were undocumented and integrally implicated in immigration issues. The U.S.C.C.B. has also served an additional 121 people who are entitled to aid, mostly as spouses or children of victims. Of the total 690 people served, 72 percent are female.

Human trafficking is lucrative for the brokers, who, like traffickers of drugs and weapons, protect their "products" because people are reusable: they can be sold and resold, over and over again.

In the Name of Security

Despite the Trafficking Victims Protection Act, a federal law passed to protect victims, implementation can become blurred when a person's status as an "undocumented person" trumps the status of "victim." Societal mantras (like "they broke the law" and "they could be terrorists") and increasing hostility toward undocumented persons also play a negative role.

Since law enforcement officers are trained primarily to be vigilant about national security, they may treat the human rights of trafficking victims as secondary. In the name of national security, they may detain and deport people who lack legal documents, often without investigating for evidence of human trafficking. At that point the cycle of trafficking may simply begin again. While some well-informed officials do the right thing by victims of trafficking, they are in a minority.

Human trafficking itself is a far greater threat to the United States than are the undocumented foreign nationals the traffickers have victimized.

At the state level, the distinctions between undocumented persons and victims of human trafficking may become even less relevant. People defined as victims by federal law may be treated at the state level as criminals. In the absence of comprehensive federal immigration reform, states have started enacting their own immigration laws. The National Conference of State Legislatures reports that 1,404 measures were introduced in states around the country between January and July 2007.

The Greater Threat

What becomes obscured in all this is that human trafficking itself is a far greater threat to the United States than are the undocumented foreign nationals the traffickers have victimized. And deporting victims simply feeds traffickers, who often operate as part of criminal networks that destabilize an area. Failure to identify the crime of human trafficking is a failure to identify the criminal whose trade in human persons for commercial sex or forced labor demoralizes society as a whole. As the number of victims escalates, so does the crime rate and the real threat to security. Criminalizing the victim is shortsighted at best.

Hidden trades like human trafficking also create an underground economy with its own complex systems of exchange, and this contributes to economic inequity and moral disorder.

As Moisés Naím, author of the recent book *Illicit*, says, "Supply and demand, risk and return, are trafficking's primary motivators." What drives traffickers are "profits and a set of values that is often impervious to moral denunciations." He adds that what we need are not "moral exhortations" but "honest analysis of the problem."

This is precisely what has been missing from our national debate on immigration. Bishop Nicholas DiMarzio of Brooklyn noted the lack of progress in his 2007 Labor Day statement:

> The debate was truly a case of "more heat than light," more passion than progress. In my view, sometimes anger trumped wisdom, myths overwhelmed facts, and slogans replaced solutions. After this debate we are a society more divided, a people more confused, and a nation unable to move forward.

Meanwhile, victims of human trafficking, who ought to be protected under U.S. law, are becoming more and more vulnerable as state laws conflict with one another. Without comprehensive immigration reform, state-generated initiatives could lead to continued double jeopardy for immigrants.

The intersection between immigration reform and the human rights of people is a risky one. As a society, we need a civil conversation that will both unite and change us for the better.

Government Corruption Can Lead to an Increase in Human Trafficking

United Nations Global Initiative to Fight Human Trafficking

The United Nations Global Initiative to Fight Human Trafficking (UN.GIFT) was launched in March 2007 to promote the global fight on human trafficking. More than 117 countries have signed the UN.GIFT-sponsored Protocol to Prevent, Suppress and Punish Trafficking in Persons, especially Women and Children.

Corruption is one of the major contributing factors to the crime of trafficking in persons. It is both an underlying root cause and a facilitating tool to carry out and sustain this illicit trade. Worse, corruption can also ensure safe havens for the profits collected as a result of human misery. Unfortunately, there has been very little exploration into the linkages of the two phenomena. When thinking of the images that join corruption and trafficking, one can easily imagine the border guard who is pocketing a few bills to not check a passport, or imagine the immigration officer who is willing to accept forged documents for a price, or the police officer who accepts a fee to turn a blind eye to a cry for help.

This sounds simple. However, the linkages between corruption and human trafficking are far more complicated and multifaceted. The international community has adopted legal frameworks to deal with each of these issues, but has not looked at how the two major international agreements can complement one another. Both the United Nations Convention against Corruption (UNCAC) and the Protocol to Prevent, Suppress and Punish Trafficking in Persons, especially

The Vienna Forum to Fight Human Trafficking (UN.GIFT B.P.:20). New York: United Nations Global Initiative to Fight Human Trafficking, 2008. Copyright © 2008 United Nations. Reprinted with the permission of the United Nations.

Women and Children deal with the issues in isolation. This forum is an opportunity to create a dialogue on how the two issues can be brought together.

Understanding Trafficking and Corruption

The Protocol against Trafficking in Persons provides the first internationally agreed upon definition of 'trafficking in persons'. According to the Protocol, the crime basically consists of three elements:

(i) Acts	such as transport, transfer, harbouring, receipt of a person,
by *(ii) Means*	of deception, coercion, abuse of a position of vulnerability and others
for *(iii)* the *Purpose of Exploitation*	including sexual exploitation, labour exploitation, removal of organs, etc.

Trafficking in persons can also be seen as a process, consisting of at least three stages, normally recruitment, transport and exploitation. An additional fourth phase would be the subsequent laundering of the proceeds of the crime. Trafficking in persons does not require an illegal border crossing and corruption can also fuel so-called internal trafficking. The Protocol against Trafficking in Persons, though supplementing the Convention against Transnational Organized Crime, also does not necessitate the illegal actions of an organized criminal group.

The most commonly-used definitions of corruption for development practitioners are probably those advanced by the World Bank and Transparency International (TI). The World Bank's working definition of corruption basically is "the abuse of public power for private benefit". TI takes a broader approach: "the misuse of entrusted power for private gain".

However, there is no single, universally-accepted definition of corruption. The UNCAC, rather than defining the phenomenon, provides a wide range of individual acts of corruption, including bribery, embezzlement of public funds, money laundering and obstruction of justice. It not only lists acts of corruption but also requires States to establish them as criminal, civil or administrative offences. The Convention addresses various areas including preventive measures, criminalization and law enforcement, international cooperation, and recovery of corruption assets.

Corruption can establish close ties between traffickers and those who are actually charged with bringing them to justice.

Many media reports focus on grand corruption, the millions stolen by corrupt political leaders. However, the cost of corruption also occurs very much at the petty levels, the few bills passed to the corrupt officials may at times dwarf the large individual corruption cases. For that reason corruption must be attacked on both fronts, especially to get control of the illicit trafficking in persons.

Corruption and Human Trafficking

Corruption can emerge before, during and after the actual trafficking crime, which means that corruption is not limited to countries of origin and transit countries, but also facilitates the continued exploitation of trafficking victims once at their destination.

Police officers, labour inspectors and others working in the field of administrative controls, health workers, NGO [non-governmental organization] staff, and other actors may be prepared to turn a blind eye to trafficking situations that come to their attention for a 'small fee'. Corrupt practices may also play a role after the actual identification and rescue of a trafficked victim, e.g. before, during and after possible criminal proceedings. Such practices are applied by the traffickers to avoid conviction and otherwise obstruct the actions of those who should assist and protect the trafficked victims and investigate, prosecute and convict the traffickers. Traffickers often have the means and feel no inhibitions against bribing their way through the criminal justice system, and investigators assigned to the case all too often fail to overcome the temptation. Corruption can establish close ties between traffickers and those who are actually charged with bringing them to justice.

Cases are known of criminal justice practitioners who back a particular trafficking ring by exclusively arraigning other, rival trafficking networks.

There are also reported instances of law enforcement officers and prosecutors demanding sexual services and financial or other payments from the victims in exchange for pursuing their case. For a trafficked person, this amounts to revictimization. There are also reports of immigration officials requesting returnees to pay them bribes.

Corruption ensures that trafficking in persons remains a low-risk, high-profit crime.

Corruption can be one of the main reasons why victims are unwilling to turn to the police and cooperate with the criminal justice system.

Also persons who are involved in victims assistance work have been reported to make their support dependent on unlawful payments from the victim. The list of possibilities for corruption to sustain the crime of trafficking in persons seems endless. . . .

It can be a vicious circle: corruption is used to facilitate the recruitment, transport and exploitation of victims of trafficking, prevent justice and ensure that the vast profits made through this inhumane criminal activity remain in the hands of the traffickers. And the very assets enable the criminals to exert even greater influence on public and private officials who actively or passively participate in trafficking in persons.

Corruption ensures that trafficking in persons remains a low-risk, high-profit crime. The prevalence and existing levels of corruption can well influence which routes the traffickers take, their *modus operandi*, and other trafficking patterns. Corruption may also result in less alertness towards the risks of trafficking: in some areas the existence of corruption is so prevalent, so omnipresent in people's everyday life that many people may not even see a difference between obtaining identification documents or a necessary travel paper legally or illegally, as one would be asked for a bribe in either case.

However, corruption not only plays a role in the actual trafficking and post-trafficking scenarios, but also with regard to the breeding grounds for trafficking in persons. Corruption, has been identified as one of the main obstacles to economic and social development. It is known to be interlinked with poverty and lack of opportunities, with insecurity, the establishment of criminal environments, the absence of the rule of law, etc., with all of these factors being among the root causes for trafficking in persons. Corruption can also play a role in the demand side of the crime, e.g. when the violation of laws and regulations on the protection of migrants and migrant workers is treated like a peccadillo [minor offense].

The Way Forward

The development of effective strategies against corruption and human trafficking require the establishment of an adequate legal and regulatory framework. Such a framework is now available at the international level in the form of the UNCAC and the Protocol against Trafficking in Persons. The existence of these instruments is a powerful manifestation of the collective political will of the international community to put in place benchmarks.

The challenge the international community is facing is to ensure that these international instruments go beyond being a sign of a mere aspiration and become functional instruments. In order to meet that challenge it is crucial to bear in mind that it is not the Government, the private sector, or civil society alone who can deal with these problems, we need to combine our efforts to curb these interrelated phenomena.

Information is key: information about the extent and linkages of the two phenomena, the *modus operandi* of the criminals involved, etc. We need to understand these linkages, considering that they will vary according to the specific context. It is also necessary to raise the awareness of all the actors that could be potentially involved in the trafficking process by means of corruption.

We also need to understand and explore the mutually reinforcing nature of the UNCAC and the Protocol against Trafficking in Persons.

At the policy level, when dealing with trafficking in persons, it is key to recognize corruption and try to formulate responses that remove this lubricant that facilitates trafficking in persons.

At the operational level, there is the need to integrate interventions in both areas of anti-corruption and anti-human trafficking. To meet this need it is important to bring together practitioners working in the areas of anti-corruption and anti-human trafficking to adopt an integrated approach when dealing with the two phenomena

Anti-corruption measures can relate to various aspects of trafficking in persons. Preventive measures should address possible corruption at the recruitment, transport and exploitation stages of trafficking, during criminal investigations of trafficking and the provision of protection of and assistance to victims.

CHAPTER 2

What Can Individuals and Organizations Do to Reduce Human Trafficking?

Chapter Preface

The United Nations International Labor Organization (ILO) estimates there are 12.3 million people worldwide in forced and bonded labor and sexual servitude. Louise Shelley, the founder and director of the Terrorism, Transnational Crime and Corruption Center (TraCCC) at George Mason University, stated at a Washington, D.C., conference on trafficking in July 2008 that of that number, approximately three hundred thousand are Americans. Due to the enormity and global nature of the problem, governments cannot battle this problem on their own. In fact, some policy makers have argued that nongovernmental organizations (NGOs) are much more effective at combating human trafficking than are governments. However, conflicts between requirements for government funding and organization philosophies have long been troubling.

In January 2009 the American Civil Liberties Union (ACLU) sued the federal government for misappropriation of funds. The ACLU charged that by giving $6 billion to the U.S. Conference of Catholic Bishops (USCCB), the federal government outwardly supported discriminatory religious doctrine, which is a violation of the separation of church and state clause in the Constitution. The ACLU claims that the USCCB refuses to use government funds to support the use of contraceptives and abortions, even among prostitutes, and that the USCCB bases its aid decisions on religious beliefs rather than on need. In a statement made shortly after the lawsuit was filed, Daniel Mach, an ACLU litigation director, asserted that "the Bush administration has sanctioned the United States Conference of Catholic Bishops' blatant misuse of taxpayer dollars. It has allowed USCCB to impose its religious beliefs on trafficking victims by prohibiting sub grantees from ensuring access to services like . . . abortion."

The USCCB and other religious organizations that reach out to victims of human trafficking argue that they must uphold their values, even when administering aid. In response to the ACLU's lawsuit, USCCB spokesperson Sister Mary Ann Walsh noted, "Everything we do has to be consistent with our beliefs." She further defended the USCCB's practices by noting the organization's effectiveness in fighting human trafficking: "The problem of trafficking in this country is huge and serious and the Catholic Church has the best network of services bar none. Going to the Catholic Church for social services is very logical." The U.S. government further supported its decision to fund the USCCB's mission by clarifying its intentions. In a 2009 article in LifeNews.com, Steve Ertlet quotes government representative Kenneth Wolfe as saying, "These federal funds are awarded with the clear purpose of caring for unaccompanied minors here from other countries . . . [not] to facilitate procuring an abortion."

Despite this controversy, NGOs continue to play a large role in fighting human trafficking. The authors in this chapter debate the effectiveness of NGOs in stamping out this global problem, including efforts to educate and organize those involved.

Human Trafficking Is as Difficult to Define as It Is to Stop

Kerry Howley

Kerry Howley is a senior editor at Reason *and a former feature editor of* Myanmar Times *in Southeast Asia.*

If you picked up, moved to Paris, and landed a job, what would you call yourself? Chances are, if you're an American, you'd soon find yourself part of a colorful community of "expats." If, while there, you hired an Algerian nanny—a woman who had picked up, moved abroad, and landed a job—how would you refer to him or her? *Expat* probably isn't the first word that springs to mind. Yet almost no one refers to herself as a "migrant worker."

Laura María Agustín's *Sex at the Margins* catalogues the many ways in which wealthy Westerners cast immigrants as The Other, and for this reason it is a profoundly uncomfortable read. Having spent many years as an educator working with expatriate sex workers, Agustín turns her attention to the "rescue industry" and the way those who would help describe the migrants they've pledged to assist.

Immigrants vs. Expatriates

Comparing the ways immigrants describe their experiences and the ways NGO [nongovernmental organization] personnel and theorists describe immigrants, she writes, "The crux of the difference concerns autonomy; whether travellers are perceived to have quite a lot versus little or none at all." Theories of migration portray migrants as unsophisticated and desperate people who are "pushed" and "pulled" along a variety of dimensions. "The tourism and pleasure seeking of people from 'developing societies', rarely figures, as though migration and tourism were mutually exclusive," she writes. "Why should the travels to work of people from less wealthy countries be supposed to differ fundamentally from those of Europeans?" Supposedly, "migrants" travel because they are poor and desperate and "expatriates" travel because they are curious, self-actualizing cosmopolites. But Agustín searches in vain for an immigrant whose self-identity reflects the wretched portrait of the model migrant drawn by those who would help.

As Agustín shows, nowhere are these human caricatures more exaggerated than in the contemporary conversation about human trafficking, or—to use a term Agustín detests—"sex trafficking." While selling sex may be a rational choice for some, governmental and charitable anti-trafficking initiatives rarely discriminate between those who would prefer sex work to the relevant alternatives and those who have been wronged. Sex slavery statistics are so tenuous that debunking them is a sport for skeptical journalists, while genuine labor abuses go ignored.

Collective anxiety about women who traverse sexual and spatial boundaries is anything but new. As Agustín writes, "Women who cross borders have long been viewed as deviant, so perhaps the present-day panic about the sexuality of women is not surprising." Immigrants are human beings with the courage to leave the comforts of home. In *Sex at the Margins*, Agustín asks readers to leave behind easy stereotypes about migrants and welcome the overlooked expats among us.

Reason spoke with Agustín in December [2007].

Reason: What experiences led you to write Sex at the Margins?

Laura María Agustín: I was working in NGOs and social projects on the Mexico/US Border, the Caribbean, and in South America. I worked with people who called themselves sex workers and gays having sex with tourists. To us, this was normal, conventional. Everyone talked about it. Obviously many of these people didn't have many options. Some of them had the guts to travel, and I felt I understood that.

[Migrants are] not the most desperate, like famine suffer-ers, who manage to undertake a migration.

In '94 I hadn't heard the word, the word *trafficking*, in this context. In the sex context, it's a creation of the past 10 years. I started running into the term when I came to Europe and saw what people who were trying to help migrants were doing and saying. The whole idea of migrants who sell sex being *victims* was so different from what I knew. My original research question was, why is there such a big difference between what people in Europe say about people who sell sex, and what those people say about themselves? It took a while for me to answer that question.

Migrants Are Widely Stereotyped

You write that migrants are considered "separate, uncreative, and unsophisticated" in theories of tourism and migration. What are we missing when we assume all migrants are simply desper-ate?

People may feel under the gun, but people who end up leaving home to work abroad have mixed motives. They may be poor and without many choices. But they also are normal human beings who have desires and fantasies. They daydream about all the same pleasurable things that richer people do. The human ability to imagine that things can be better, that getting ahead is possible, is in play. These motivations mix to-gether in the project of leaving home—legally or not—to go somewhere else.

And it's not the most desperate, like famine sufferers, who manage to undertake a migration. In order to go abroad you have to be healthy and you have to have social capital, including a network that will get you information on how to travel and work. You need some money and some names and addresses; you have to have at least some official papers, even if they're false. You need at least a minimal safety net. People at the most disadvantaged social level rarely get into this situation.

The U.N. protocols on trafficking and smuggling of human beings are gendered.

How are attitudes about trafficking related to the idea that women shouldn't be leaving home in the first place?

Women are sometimes called "boundary markers": When States feel threatened, women's bodies become symbols of home and the nation. This is a common sexist idea in patriarchal societies. The idea that women are domestic and symbolize home and hearth—but also that they should *stay* home and *be* home—is deeply entrenched all over the world. And while richer countries might favour gender equity for their *own* women, they often "domesticate" women from poorer contexts.

The U.N. protocols on trafficking and smuggling of human beings are gendered, the trafficking protocol mentions women and children, and mentions sexual exploitation, but doesn't say anything about voluntary, leaving. The smuggling protocol talks about men who want to travel but have crossed a border in a less than kosher way—and sex is not mentioned.

People talk about a contemporary "feminization" of migration, but the evidence for this is shaky. There have been other waves of women migrating in numbers, as in the late 19th century from Europe to Argentina, where they were often accused of being prostitutes. Europeans didn't want to think these white women would set out on their own like this or end up selling sex, which is where the term "white slavery" derives from. The phenomenon was similar to what we see to-day, only the direction has shifted.

Trafficking Badly Defined and Exaggerated

What do you make of the State Department's claim that 800,000 people are trafficked each year?

Numbers like this are fabricated by defining trafficking in an extremely broad way to take in enormous numbers of people. The Office to Monitor and Combat Trafficking in Persons is using the widest possible definition, which assumes that *any* woman who sells sex could not really want to, and, if she crossed a national border, she was forced.

The numbers are egregious partly because the research is cross-cultural. The US, calling itself the world's moral arbiter on these issues, uses its embassies in other countries to talk to the police and other local authorities, supposedly to find out how many people were trafficked. There is a language issue—all the words involved don't translate perfectly, and there is a confusion about what *trafficking* means. People don't all use it the same way. Even leaving aside language issues, we know the data aren't being collected using a standard methodology across countries. 800,000 is a fantasy number.

I believe [governments] are less concerned about women "victims" than male "perpetrators."

Is there a legitimate core of abuses that need to be addressed?

Some conscientious people talk about trafficking as applicable to men, transsexuals, or anyone you like, no matter what kind of work they do, when things go very wrong during a migration. When migrants are charged egregious amounts of money they can't possibly pay back, for example. However, we've reached the point in this cultural madness where most people *mean specifically* women who sell sex when they use the word "trafficking." They usually mean women working inside brothels.

So there is an attempt to conflate the terms prostitution and trafficking?

There is a definite effort to conflate the terms in a stream of feminism I call "fundamentalist feminism." These feminists believe there is a single definition of Woman, and that sexual experience is key to a woman's life, soul, self-definition. This particular group has tried to say that prostitution is not only by definition exploitation but *is* trafficking. It's bizarre but they are maintaining that.

Fundamentalists' Legal Objectives

What about the fundamentalist fundamentalists?

The alliance between fundamentalist feminists and some fundamentalist Christians sees its work as global. So you get the Southern Baptist Convention and some feminists writing to the government of the Czech Republic to urge against legalizing prostitution. Many kinds of fundamentalist thought share values about home, family, sex, and violence.

Are anti-trafficking activists preventing the liberalization of prostitution laws?

Probably. But I don't think the obsession with trafficking is solely about women and sex. It's become a cultural phenomenon up in the stratosphere with fears of terrorism. Governments are making it an issue of policing the borders, and I believe they are less concerned about women "victims" than male "perpetrators." The UN protocols on trafficking and smuggling were attached to a convention on organized crime. It's the same as the terrorism story, the idea that bad guys don't respect States and will set up their own societies, go where they want and disobey all laws. The borders will not hold, the martians are invading. Everything is Falling Apart.

Is there a romanticization of home at work here? The idea that it's always best to stay in the place you come from?

Immigration procedures still assume that everyone calls some country "home", but many people's situations don't easily fit this idea. They've got more than one home or don't want to call anyplace home. The collective fantasy says home is always a lovely place, but many people have a contrary experience. People who actually *want* to leave home may feel they have failed—whether they were leaving behind their parents, partner or children.

You write: "Believing passionately that women must tell their stories is a governmental urge."

When I started studying, I thought it would be easy: Why not listen to what migrants themselves say? Then I found an enormous literature, much of it explicitly feminist, urging subjects to speak authentically, to get up and tell their true stories for everyone to hear. With all kinds of marginalized people, the idea was they've been silenced and should be allowed to speak.

Except it turns out that lots of people don't want to tell their stories, they don't want to stand up anywhere, they'd just as soon let someone speak for them. Or they don't care or know they are being talked about, they just want to do whatever they feel like doing. So I had to question my own desire to push people to present themselves in a certain kind of way. It's not enough to say, "we will facilitate people giving voice." No, because also that gives *us* a job. Then we can see our job as being a virtuous person who is going to help the poor and silenced of the earth speak.

It's also not clear that they would get anything out of speaking, because governments, and most people, don't listen when they do. Those who see themselves as helping believe they Know Best how we should all live and benevolently provide necessary services to us all.

Investigators Are Looking for a Bad Guy

Both the U.N. and U.S. have promoted the idea that human trafficking is perpetrated by organized crime rings. How accurate is this?

The Interpols and FBIs of the world are trying to find out exactly who the bad guys are who are doing the trafficking. They have a terrible time of it, because trafficking in the sense that they mean includes most irregular migration. Millions and millions of people are involved, most of them working on a small scale—petty criminals, not big-time mafiosi. I lived in Spain for five years and at least once every week the media carried a story about the police breaking up a trafficking ring—which means there are always more and more.

But there's no evidence that large-scale organized crime has gone into human trafficking the way they did into heroin trafficking decades ago. What researchers have found is small-scale operations—people who know one person they can call in Berlin and one in Istanbul, who use mobile phones, who move around. Small-time entrepreneurs, some meaner, some acting like regular travel agents.

What policies would you recommend for people concerned about legitimately coercive situations?

I'm trying to get people to slow down on the rush to determine a definitive policy. Because the prostitution debate is so limited and moralistic, vast amounts of information that policymakers need is still absent. Research on traffickers themselves is just beginning. The diversity of experience is enormous. There isn't going to be a single social policy that will work for everyone.

Educating Johns About Forced Prostitution Can Help Reduce Demand

Miyoko Ohtake

Miyoko Ohtake is associate editor at Dwell Magazine *and a former reporter for the San Francisco bureau of* Newsweek.

It's after 11 a.m. when Emmanuelle, an attractive 41-year-old former prostitute dressed in a red-and-black V-neck dress, takes the podium at San Francisco's Hall of Justice. She's clearly very nervous, but that's not surprising. In another time and place, the 40 or so men sitting in rows of plastic upholstered chairs might have been her customers. In fact they're here on a warm Saturday in May because they've been arrested for trying to buy sex.

Fighting the Exploitation of Women

The men, who are diverse in age and ethnicity, are voluntarily taking part in something called the First Offender Prostitution Program (FOPP). It's a bit like traffic school for drivers with too many speeding tickets. But the day's lineup at what is sometimes called "johns school" has a unique curriculum—a series of "scared straight" talks about the ills of prostitution mixed with some seriously graphic sexual-health education. By attending the eight-hour session, and paying a $1,000 fee, these "johns" can avoid being prosecuted for solicitation. More than 5,700 men have gone through the program since its inception in March 1995. Over the last decade, the number of arrests annually in San Francisco for soliciting sex has varied widely, ranging from 140 to 1,200.

San Francisco's johns school is part of a renewed nationwide push by law enforcement to focus more on the buyers of sex than the sellers—a method that, if initial studies are to be believed, seems to be more effective than the cops' periodic roundups of prostitutes. Thirty-nine other U.S. cities have similar education programs in place, most based on San Francisco's school, which got government support after a city task force on prostitution created in 1994 recommended that officials focus on the social issues fueling prostitution instead of prosecution.

Now, the future of the johns school is in question. [In July 2008], supporters of a measure to decriminalize prostitution announced that they had enough signatures to get the initiative on the ballot [that] fall. The bill, backed by the Erotic Service Providers Union [ESPU], a San Francisco-based labor group, would not only end arrests for solicitation and prostitution, but also contains a specific provision that would prevent the city from funding the First Offenders program. [*Editor's note:* In November 2008, San Francisco voters rejected this initiative.]

Programs like the johns school help sensitize those who buy sexual services to the true working conditions of sex workers.

"Criminalizing sex workers has been putting workers at risk of violence and discrimination for far too long," said Maxine Doogan of the ESPU, in a statement July 18 [2008]. The group believes that city resources are being wasted in they call "a futile effort to police consensual sex between adults."

But San Francisco Mayor Gavin Newsom and the city's district attorney, Kamala D. Harris, strongly disagree. "To suggest that this is somehow an issue that only involves consensual adults, that's just not true. No matter how these girls and women are packaged for sale, the reality is that for many of them, their life experience is often wrought with abuse and exploitation," says Harris. The proposed measure would hamper efforts to crack down on human trafficking, she says, because it prevents police resources from being used to locate and help immigrant women and children in particular who have been forced into sex work by traffickers who lure them to the United States with promises of other kinds of employment.

Harris says that programs like the johns school help sensitize those who buy sexual services to the true working conditions of sex workers—and refute the notion that many of them are in the business voluntarily. "It forces the john to deal with the reality of prostitution instead of their fantasy of what's happening," she says.

If you want to tackle prostitution and trafficking, you have to start with demand reduction.

Dismantling the Fantasy

Dismantling that fantasy is precisely what Emmanuelle and several other ex-sex workers have come to the johns school to do. Emmanuelle (who requested that *Newsweek* not use her real name in print) explains that the women she worked with were often mentally and physically ill. "I have posttraumatic stress disorder from [the work]," she says. "I want to be one of those people who has a good job, a long marriage. But because of my illness, I'm scarred for life from this industry, and I have to restart my life at 41." By the time she finishes telling the men about her life on the street, many of the men in the room are openly weeping or sniffling. They applaud as she walks away and another ex-prostitute, Jenna, 33, takes the stage to tell her story.

Jenna, a 33-year-old redhead, started working as a cigarette vendor at a club as a teen. She tells the men that she "didn't start off wanting to be a prostitute" but that the attention she got from men at nightspots and a $200-a-day heroin addiction she developed helped propel her into that lifestyle. Soon, Jenna (who declined to provide her last name) would find herself homeless and infected with hepatitis C, the victim of repeated beatings by abusive clients. Now, she says, even though she's been out of the sex industry for three years, she can't maintain a relationship with a guy longer than a few weeks. "I'm damaged, but it has to be true for some of you, too," she says to the johns. "You don't realize when you're getting yourself off what you're doing to these women. You're causing a lot of damage. We're damaged, but you guys are, too."

And they work hard for the money. According to a preliminary report released this year by researchers at the University of Chicago, based on a study of prostitution in Chicago from Aug. 19, 2005 to May 1, 2007, a streetwalker makes on average $27 per hour; given the limited hours prostitutes normally work, this would generate less than $20,000 annually. The women also reported frequent physical abuse. According to the study, a woman working on the street could expect an annual average of a dozen acts of violence and 300 instances of unprotected sex.

The johns school was founded by Norma Hotaling, a 56-year-old ex-prostitute who founded FOPP in 1995; she also launched an umbrella group, SAGE (Standing Against Global Exploitation), which combats sex trafficking and helps those trapped in the trade get out and find mainstream jobs. Both organizations aim to put pressure on the other people involved in the prostitution transaction.... "It's taken until now to realize there are men involved," Hotaling says. "But if you want to tackle prostitution and trafficking, you have to start with demand reduction."

That's where the johns school seems to be having an effect. The San Francisco program shows it is possible to appeal to the customers' sense of "empathy for those harmed," says Michael Shively, a sociologist who reviewed the program for the Department of Justice, which provides some of its funding. Shively's study, released in May [2008], found that recidivism rates of those who completed johns school were 30 percent less likely to be rearrested for soliciting sex than were men who did not opt for the program. And an earlier study of a similar program in Buffalo, N.Y., resulted in an 87.5 percent drop in the recidivism rate for attendees. Shively admits he was skeptical at first. "It didn't seem realistic that one eight-hour day of talking at men would change their behavior," he says. "Now I'm an advocate."

The Many Sides to Legalization

The johns school attendees are mainly men who've tried to hire women who work the street—rather than those who have sought the services of the growing indoor prostitution trade (escort services, sensual massage parlors, etc.). The indoor trade is sometimes viewed as less perilous for the prostitutes involved, and the data on them is less comprehensive. However, a recent study by researchers at Columbia University found that while sex workers in this category experience lower rates of physical violence, these women are more vulnerable because assaults happen off the radar. These prostitutes, according to study authors Sudhir Venkatesh and Alexandra Murphy, tend to be "invisible" and often become isolated from their community and from other women in the trade who might provide a social network. That's one reason escorts find it hard to leave the business.

U.S. law-enforcement officials have also found a link between human trafficking and prostitution.

Some advocates say that legalization would help bring these women and others like them out of the shadows and destigmatize the profession. And, according to San Francisco's Erotic Service Providers Union, decriminalizing the profession would allow these women to fight for better working conditions and pay and would make it easier for sex workers to report crimes without fear of prosecution themselves. But anti-prostitution activists point to studies indicating that legalizing prostitution may in fact create an environment that encourages human trafficking and pushes violence and abuse against sex workers even further underground.

A 2007 study by San Francisco psychologist and prostitution expert Melissa Farley found that in places where commercial sex is legal—such as Nevada, Germany, Australia and the Netherlands—illegal prostitution, as well as the number of rapes and assaults against prostitutes, has increased. Farley also found that more than 80 percent of the women working as prostitutes in Nevada's legal brothels "urgently want to escape." Both Germany and the Netherlands—country infamous for their red-light districts—are reconsidering their decisions to legalize the practice.

U.S. law-enforcement officials have also found a link between human trafficking and prostitution. The House passed an anti-human-trafficking bill in 2007 that would lower the barriers for prosecuting johns and traffickers, but it faces serious opposition in the Senate. (More than 800,000 people are trafficked across international borders each year, according to U.S. officials. Of those, 80 percent are female and about 50 percent are children.)

The idea that some of the women selling sexual services might in reality be young girls is another concept that the johns school hopes to impart to its "students." District Attorney Harris estimates that there are as many as a thousand girls under 18 working San Francisco's streets.

One participant in the johns-school program, "Anthony," was getting a crash course in some of these truths. A 45-year-old paralegal recently laid off from his job, he wound up in the program after he tried to pick up an undercover officer working in the city's seedy Tenderloin district. He admits that he'd paid for sex before in Tijuana, Mexico. But after hearing a lecture at johns school about children in the sex industry, he swore he was finished. "I never thought that I could be picking up a child who looks 22 or 23 but is really under 18," he told *Newsweek*. "The possibility of ruining a child's life . . . I'm never putting myself in that situation again." [The men interviewed declined to provide their real names owing to the sensitive nature of the subject.] "Marco," another arrested john in the class, didn't think he had much to learn at the start of the eight-hour session. "Aside from knowledge of the vice unit and how they operate, everything else I already know," he said. But at 4 p.m., the 23-year-old construction worker found himself leaving with more than the papers certifying his completion of the course; he also had a Sex Addicts Anonymous meeting schedule tucked under his arm. "I was going through the list, and I fit a lot of the criteria of a sex addict," he said. "I thought it was a rare thing, but I might check out a class."

Outreach Organizations Can Decrease Child Trafficking

Lisa Tsering

Lisa Tsering is a staff reporter for India-West *and a regular contributor to the* Hollywood Reporter.

Rani was just seven when she was plunged into the dark world of human trafficking.

Her family, who lived in a small South Indian village outside Chennai, loved their little girl very much, but they had other mouths to feed and they were struggling to make ends meet. So when a neighborhood woman offered to take her in, and promised her food, clothes and an education, they felt it was a positive step for their little girl.

What they didn't realize was that the woman was a recruiter for human traffickers; when her mother went to visit one day, she was shocked to find that little Rani had vanished.

It was the beginning of over a year of terror, pain and despair for Rani.

"I have tears more than anyone can know," Rani, now married with two children, told *India-West* January 9 [2008] by phone from Olympia, Washington.

Although Rani has blacked out the worst memories, she remembers crying for her mother over and over again, being shuttled from one place to the next by cruel handlers in the slave trade who severely beat and abused her, and finding herself in towns where no one spoke her language.

"Telling my story is difficult," she said. "No one wants to relive that. But I know that I came through it, and I want to be a voice for those voiceless children."

Former Victims Save Others

After being sold into slavery, Rani was so traumatized that she became physically and mentally ill. Covered in scars and sores, she would hardly speak. At one point, her broker decided that in her condition she couldn't bring in enough income, so he sold her on the black market. She ended up in an orphanage, and by a stroke of luck was adopted by an American family.

At the age of eight, in 1979, Rani came to the United States, and her remarkable adventure began.

> *The shelter [offers] not just a safe and welcome home, but also services that trafficking victims need to start rebuilding their lives.*

One year later, a nine-year-old boy from Vietnam named Trong Hong—also a victim of human trafficking and torture—was adopted in Washington state. Later, in high school, Trong and Rani met on a blind date. They eventually fell in love and married.

Today, Rani and Trong Hong run the Tronie Foundation, a center in Olympia, Washington, that aims to stop modern day slavery by performing outreach and working with lawmakers and law enforcement. They also own Tronie Homes, a company that designs and builds luxury homes.

In February [2008], the Tronie Foundation [opened] a shelter for trafficking victims that Rani believes is one of the first of its kind in the country. Based in a remodeled five-bedroom home in an undisclosed location, the shelter will offer not just a safe and welcome home, but also services that trafficking victims need to start rebuilding their lives, such as job training and life skills. "It's more than just a place for rescues," she told *India-West*. "We want it to be a home."

The opening of the shelter [coincided] with National Freedom Day February 1, a holiday proclaimed by President Harry Truman in 1948 to promote equal opportunity and freedom in the United States.

Modern-day slavery is one of the largest criminal activities in the world, outranked only by drugs and arms-dealing.

Many of the victims of human trafficking Rani encounters in Washington have come from the Asia-Pacific region. "But we see a lot from India, too," she said.

Rani urges Indian Americans to stay aware of human trafficking within their own communities. "Tell people there is an issue. Stop this crime from happening," she said.

According to a statement from the Tronie Foundation, approximately 1.2 million children are trafficked each year around the world. Between 50 and 60 percent of the children who are trafficked into sexual slavery are under the age of 16. Statistics also demonstrate that between 600,000 to 800,000 persons are victims of human trafficking across international borders, and many others fall victim within their own territory. In the United States, around 14,500 to 17,500 are trafficked within its borders.

Activists such as those at the Polaris Project and the Contemporary Slavery Institute claim that modern-day slavery is one of the largest criminal activities in the world, outranked only by drugs and arms-dealing.

A Long Way Yet to Go

Rani and her husband push for laws at the state and national level that will protect victims and increase prosecution of offenders. "The laws are okay, but could have some improvement," she said. "They're doing great making laws, but we have to enforce them. I'd rather see us enforce the laws we've already created."

The United States Department of Health and Human Services ensures that victims of trafficking who are non-U.S. citizens may be eligible for a special "T visa," which awards certain benefits and services under any federal or state program or activity to the same extent as a refugee.

Rani's home of Washington state, which is a hotbed of trafficking activity, is one of 33 states with anti-trafficking criminal provisions. The state also has an anti-trafficking task force and victim protection provisions in place.

But Rani and Trong know that each victim's story is unique. That's why in addition to advocating for policy changes, the couple works with victims one-on-one, to listen to their stories.

Some victims are part of mail-order bride schemes, while others are sold into servitude or sexual slavery. Some, like Rani, were exploited by international adoption rings.

"My adoptive mother didn't know my past," Rani explained. "All she was told was that I'd been abandoned to an orphanage and that my parents had died. She didn't know I was kidnapped."

Rani's story took an even more extraordinary turn when she finally returned to India in 1999, after 21 years away.

Through an intensive investigation, she was able to track down her birth mother, whom she'd been told was dead. Her mother, too, had assumed that Rani was dead.

"I met my entire family," she said, declining to give her family's name or the name of the town, to protect their privacy. "It was a huge reunion. Imagine, seeing someone you didn't even know was alive. I imagine my brother and sisters' pain, when their sister was gone, and they had no idea what had happened to me. That's why I say this should never happen in today's society," she told *India-West*.

"I waited for someone else to tell the story. Nobody did. We are very few, the people who come forward."

Outreach Organizations Have a Limited Impact on Reducing Child Trafficking

Mike Ceaser

Mike Ceaser is a journalist based in Bogota, Colombia. His work has appeared in the Christian Science Monitor, *the* San Francisco Chronicle, *and many other publications.*

Police-car lights flashed and prostitutes, pimps, reporters, and police officers milled about. One by one, the neon signs displaying scantily clad women went dark. Finally, the police sealed the gates beneath the billboard of two naked women amid the moon and stars.

While the police closed the La Luna nightclub [in Ecuador] for employing underage girls as prostitutes, a pair of graduate students from Dominican University, near Chicago, stood by urging them on. For the students, the shuttering of the club was a personal victory.

"I don't think that prostitution can be a choice that you make," said Tracy O'Dowd, who, along with Sergio Velarde, had assisted in winning the court battle against the owners of the nightclub. "I think you're brought there one way or another."

Understanding the Sex Trade

Ms. O'Dowd and Mr. Velarde, both master's-degree students in social work, had come here three months earlier, in late January [2008], to work as interns at the Our Youth Foundation, which is based in Ecuador and battles the exploitation of children. Concerned about human trafficking and interested

Mike Ceaser, "A Dark Window on Human Trafficking," *Chronicle of Higher Education,* vol. 54, July 25, 2008, p. A5. Copyright © 2008 by The Chronicle of Higher Education. This article may not be published, reposted, or redistributed without express permission from The Chronicle.

in Latin America, both had studied the issue of trafficking at Dominican. Before leaving home, they learned that the sexual exploitation of minors was common in Ecuador, and that the country's corrupt and inefficient legal system rarely took action against those responsible.

Only in 2005 did Ecuador pass its first major law against human trafficking; in 2007 the United States' "Trafficking in Persons Report" said that Ecuador "does not fully comply with the minimum standards for the elimination of trafficking," though the report also noted improvements in prosecutions, public education, and support for victims.

Mr. Velarde, whose parents and grandparents emigrated from Mexico to the United States, speaks passionately about the challenges faced by migrants, who are often exploited even when they are not the victims of traffickers. Once, while visiting relatives in the Mexican state of Chihuahua, his family encountered immigrants from Central America who had been abandoned there and told they were in the United States. The many fast-food restaurants made the locale resemble a U.S. city.

Mr. Velarde believes that in "individualistic" American society, people are leery of supporting and assisting immigrants—even those who were brought to the United States against their will.

Sometimes young men seek out girls from poor, troubled families and pretend to fall in love with them—and then "sell" them to brothel owners.

"Once the stigma is placed on immigrants, it doesn't matter how you got there," Mr. Velarde says. "If you got there on your free will or against your free will, you're always going to have that stigma."

An Invisible Crime

But he and Ms. O'Dowd found that human trafficking in Ecuador differs fundamentally from what they'd read about in other nations, and soon found themselves swept up in a landmark legal battle against traffickers. Human trafficking generally refers to the carrying of people across borders deceitfully or against their will, for prostitution or forced labor. While that happens to Ecuadoreans, here the crime most commonly consists of forcing young girls into brothels, through coercion or outright kidnapping. Sometimes young men seek out girls from poor, troubled families and pretend to fall in love with them—and then "sell" them to brothel owners.

"Here, they do this whole fantasy couple, fantasy relationship, and then all of a sudden, 'I don't have any more money, so you have to work,'" says Mr. Velarde. "But the girl still believes they're a couple, and he still kind of treats them as a couple."

It's an often-invisible crime.

Mr. Velarde says that in his visits to poor communities, he discovered that people often don't know that such cases involve human trafficking, or are so poor that they assume their absent daughters must be better off.

Most families never imagine that their daughters have ended up at a place like La Luna, a complex of three huge nightclub-brothels, which had come to represent both the crime and the legal invulnerability often enjoyed by the perpetrators. Adult prostitution is legal in Ecuador, but La Luna was notorious for employing underage girls. In January 2006, pressured by the Our Youth Foundation and others, the police finally raided the club and rescued 11 girls, ages 13 through 17, who were taken to a safe house operated by the foundation.

The trial of the club's five owners, repeatedly postponed, dragged on until this March [2008]. Ms. O'Dowd and Mr. Velarde met three of the victims, now ages 15 through 17, when the girls prepared to testify for the prosecution. Then the two demonstrated in front of the courthouse in support of the victims—and faced off against a group backing the brothel owners.

"We stood outside the courtroom for three hours," Ms. O'Dowd wrote in the blog she posted as part of her course work. "There were about 50 people there to support these girls, and there were about 20 supporting the traffickers. We waited with posters saying 'No to sexual exploitation,' 'Justice that comes late isn't justice.'"

The crime's roots lie in the city's poor and socially troubled barrios.

In the first days of April, the court issued its verdict: All the men were guilty.

"The five men on trial were sentenced to 16 years," Mr. Velarde blogged on April 4, "and it was a huge win."

Children's-rights advocates called the club's shuttering a landmark because of its size and wealth. And officials present at the closing vowed that it was the start of a crackdown on brothels employing minors.

The Roots of Human Trafficking

But while La Luna became the face of exploitation here, the crime's roots lie in the city's poor and socially troubled barrios. And it was there that the Dominican interns did the nitty-gritty and often frustrating work intended to prevent the children of vulnerable families from ever being misled into prostitution.

The interns did this in places like a nondescript neighborhood of brick and concrete houses that Ms. O'Dowd visited one overcast day.

She knocked on the door of a home where the father had been imprisoned for sexually abusing one of his daughters.

Then, surrounded by children, Ms. O'Dowd sat on a couch with the mother in the tidy living room and asked about the family's situation and needs: How were they doing financially? Did the children need notebooks for school? Would they like counseling? But the woman seemed resigned and hopeless. Between sobs, she described how the absence of her husband, an auto mechanic, had left the family financially devastated. She was even hostile to the Our Youth Foundation, which she blamed for taking him away.

"What I want is for you to help me, to get my husband out of jail," she pleaded.

Ms. O'Dowd left feeling frustrated by the mother's attitude and lack of appreciation for the danger to her daughters.

Even united families face the threat of trafficking because of the poverty and social dislocation caused by Ecuador's heavy migration from the countryside to the wealthier cities.

Even united families face the threat of trafficking because of the poverty and social dislocation caused by Ecuador's heavy migration from the countryside to the wealthier cities.

Another morning, Mr. Velarde rode a series of buses and then a pickup truck up a dirt road to a neighborhood of crude homes scattered among bushes on a mountainside high above Quito, the capital. In a house of uninsulated brick and concrete lived an indigenous family who had migrated from the coast in search of work. The mother cleans houses when pain from a kidney stone permits, while the children's stepfather earns about $30 per month as a security guard.

Inside the home, Mr. Velarde and an intern from an Ecuadorean university interviewed the family and left satisfied that they were making do with their limited resources. But while the group waited for a bus back down the mountainside, the mother unexpectedly mentioned that two years earlier her

daughter, now 14 years old, was kidnapped by a family acquaintance, who raped her and held her captive for eight days
while trying to "sell" her to a brothel.

Although the family succeeded in rescuing the girl, she is
still afraid to leave the house. Then the mother described how
the local schoolteacher accosts female students, forcing the
family to send their daughters to a more distant school—
which means a perilous walk back home every evening.

"Sometimes I think about the other girls who are getting
bigger," their mother worried, "that the same thing could happen to them."

The interns reported the family's situation to the foundation, for follow-up assistance. "That her daughter was kidnapped—that just changes the whole situation," Mr. Velarde
observed afterward. "Research says that if they've had such a
thing with a sister, a cousin, . . . then they're vulnerable."

An Uneasy Future

Ms. O'Dowd and Mr. Velarde returned to Chicago feeling
hopeful that Ecuador was taking real steps against trafficking,
through both police actions and new laws.

But the court case against the club fell short of being a
complete victory: The owners' sentences were slashed from 16
years to six.

Their Ecuadorean experience left the Dominican students
with hopes of continuing to fight human trafficking, either in
the United States, where they feel the problem has received
too little attention, or back in Latin America. But the visit to
Ecuador also changed them both, making them more interested in preventing the circumstances that make people vulnerable to trafficking. Although thousands of people are believed to be victims of human trafficking into the United
States each year, the United States does not include itself in its
own annual trafficking report.

"As a country, I think we've focused more on everyone else," says Mr. Velarde, "and when you have eyes on everybody else, you don't have eyes on your own situation."

Prostitute Alliances Can Combat Human Trafficking

Sarah Stuteville and Alex Stonehill

Sarah Stuteville and Alex Stonehill are executive editors and journalists for The Common Language Project, a nonprofit multimedia production house that reports on social justice issues from around the world.

The smells of jasmine perfume, fried food, bidi [cigarette] smoke, and liquored breath mingle in the thick humid air. Watery pink and white neon lights from the Hotel Welcome, Dream House and Love Lotus shine in the eyes of women lined up in turquoise saris or red miniskirts and the customers jostling to admire them. Backlit in shadowy doorways, young girls beckon into the night with childish voices that betray their pre-pubescence, despite alluring gestures and deep purple lipstick.

Suddenly the mood shifts here in Sonagachi, Kolkata's [formerly, Calcutta, India's] largest red-light district, as an angry chant rises from the far end of the narrow street. The girls scramble to cover their faces with flimsy scarves and pimps in lungis and tank tops rush to their sides as thousands of women round the corner. Illuminated by torches that billow black smoke into the inky sky, the women stride forward with arms linked and scream, "We demand sex workers' rights!" and "George Bush, you can take our funds but you cannot take our fight," as they hold high a straw effigy of [then–U.S. president George W.] Bush.

Getting Organized

The tradition of Kolkata sex workers taking control of their lives is as old as its first redlight district. Five miles away, in the slums surrounding the Kalighat temple, one of the holiest sites in Hinduism, lies the birthplace of the city's sex industry. Hundreds of years ago, widows and other socially outcast women would migrate here hoping for room and board from temple priests. While they were given a little food and a place on the floor to sleep, resident priests and upper-caste men who visited the temple often required sex as payment. Recognizing that demand for sex far exceeded the returns they received, these women began a community alongside the temple and started charging for their services, and organized prostitution was born.

While media attention on sex work in Asia often focuses on underage trafficking and slavery, it is more subtle social factors that push many women into the trade. The fight for legalization of prostitution as a means to expose trafficking, as well as improve the lives of sex workers, is usually ignored.

"It's better to have a bad reputation than to be considered virtuous and be beaten every day," says Arti Pandey, 22 (name changed on request). Her story illustrates how prostitution can be a refuge from abusive families and limited economic options.

One Woman's Story

At 14, Pandey was married off to a man 20 years her senior who had designs on inheriting her ailing father's government job and a cut of his pension. When another sister's husband got the position instead, the abuse began. After learning that her husband was plotting to tie her up and feed her into a fan as retribution, Pandey ran away and began to support herself through a series of nursing and housekeeping jobs. But everywhere she went threats and demands for money followed, and her angry in-laws succeeded in getting her fired from every stable situation she found in Kolkata.

A trip to Mumbai [formerly, Bombay] changed the course of her life. There she met a friend who was working in a brothel and encouraged her to do the same. The wages the friend earned along with the promise of meeting interesting foreign men enticed her, and within months she was making a decent living. When a police raid returned her to Kolkata 18 months later, she attempted to resume "legitimate" work in a low-paying garment factory. But her in-laws soon found her out and began insisting that she return to them, for what Pandey saw as a life of further abuse and slavery.

"I realized that if I was going to live on my own I would have to return to the trade," a move that would sever her ties to mainstream society and by extension the in-laws. "This is one way you can choose to live your life, if you don't mind the work you can make a good living."

Last summer [2005] Pandey met a former sex worker turned peer educator for New Light, a non-governmental organization (NGO) that provides support for sex workers and their families. The woman helped her find a room, set her up as an independent operator in Kalighat and introduced Pandey to the organization. At New Light's office in the heart of the Kalighat red-light district, she receives regular check-ups, learns about safe sex practices, gets free condoms and has access to counselors and childcare. Even more important is the sense of non-judgmental support that the community of sex workers centered around New Light provides.

Removing the Stigma

Back in Sonagachi, the Durbar Mahila Samanwaya Committee (Unstoppable Women's Alliance Committee) is taking a more militant approach to the problems facing sex workers. The organization is made up of current or former sex workers and their families and lobbies aggressively for the legalization of prostitution.

Current law does not explicitly state that prostitution is illegal, but criminalizes solicitation and the running of brothels or renting rooms to sex workers. The Women's Alliance maintains that any criminalization of sex work reinforces harmful stigmas, creates a black market where child prostitution and trafficking can thrive and promotes a climate where the protection of women who work within the industry cannot be ensured.

The lack of programs to provide exit strategies from the trade does not address the socio-economic forces that lead women into sex work.

A new Indian law under consideration as an amendment to the Immoral Traffic Prevention Act seeks to prosecute the customers of prostitutes. Such criminalization and localized police raids in red-light districts have been linked to a decrease in condom use as the resulting scarcity of customers forces impoverished sex workers to agree to abusive or unsafe sex in order to support themselves.

Another concern is the insistence on language that equates prostitution with trafficking, denying the important role that of-age and by-choice sex workers can play in its eradication. The Women's Alliance has organized sex workers in red-light districts throughout the state of West Bengal and set up self-regulatory boards to oversee conditions in these communities in an attempt to improve wages and root out child prostitution and trafficking.

The Women's Alliance is not immune to criticism, and visible child prostitution on the streets that surround its main office is an obvious indicator of the limitations of self-regulation. It is estimated that one-third of the 9,000 prostitutes in Sonagachi are under 18.

The lack of programs to provide exit strategies from the trade does not address the socio-economic forces that lead women into sex work, and an unsettling conflict of interest is presented when the leadership of an organization profits from the business it is attempting to reform and regulate.

Despite these concerns, the Women's Alliance is the most active and influential sex workers' organization in West Bengal. The loyalty it inspires is clear in the family-like atmosphere of its offices and the banners and signs carrying its logo that are displayed throughout Sonagachi. Its ability to mobilize thousands of women from one of the most vulnerable sectors of Indian society to march proudly through the streets to demand their rights is proof of the trust the group has earned and the movement it has ignited.

[Women's alliances] have proven effective in promoting safe sex and slowing the spread of HIV and AIDS.

As dynamic as the movement for sex workers rights in Kolkata has become, its success still may rest on outside forces.

Abstinence First

The Bush administration has begun to cut funding from international organizations that condone prostitution and don't promote abstinence as a first defense against HIV and AIDS. The strengthening alliance between the U.S. and Indian governments has sparked fears that Indian laws will move to further criminalize prostitution, and the possibility of diminished international aid looms over projects like the Women's Alliance and New Light. Now it is not only the stigma of family and social disapproval sex workers must endure, but also the moralizing of a government and people that they will never meet.

For those working on the ground in places like Sonagachi or Kalighat, the first concern is that funding cuts and further criminalization will simply drive the sex trade deeper underground. While the Bush administration has been lauded for its efforts to abolish sex trafficking, organizations like the

Women's Alliance and New Light often provide the only over-sight in communities where women and children are being trafficked.

Furthermore, these programs have proven effective in promoting safe sex and slowing the spread of HIV and AIDS. Women's Alliance statistics report current condom use in Sonagachi at 89 percent and HIV infection rates among sex workers has stabilized at around 5 percent.

"We are the gatekeepers," says Roma Devnath, supervisor for the Women's Alliance Anti-Trafficking Project and a second-generation sex worker, "If you eliminate us, then HIV and AIDS will spread to the whole of society. Eventually it will even spread to the society of George Bush himself."

Despite Abolitionist Efforts, Human Trafficking Thrives

Priya Abraham

Priya Abraham, a former reporter for World Magazine, *is director of communications at the Institute on Religion and Public Policy in Washington, D.C.*

Premila's parents sold their daughter for $18 on her 18th birthday. The buyer, from hundreds of miles away, said his Indian village had no good women to marry so he had to buy a wife. He took Premila as a concubine, then sold her into 10 grinding years of prostitution in two cities before rescuers returned the shattered woman to her home.

Premila is a modern slave, one of 27 million in the world today. Two hundred years ago, slaves were relatively scarce, expensive, and publicly owned by men holding title deeds to them. Today, they are plentiful and cheap like Premila—and much harder to spot.

This week [in February 2007] Western countries celebrate the life of William Wilberforce, the pioneering abolitionist who labored 20 years to end the British slave trade, a fight he won on February 23, 1807. Today's abolitionists are no less tenacious but find their work is different: Unlike in Wilberforce's time, slavery is illegal almost everywhere. Yet modern slavery flourishes because corrupt governments and law enforcers do not enforce the law.

Modern-Day Slavery

The type of slavery Wilberforce and his American contemporaries knew was chattel slavery, in which one man owned another human being. According to the abolitionist group Free

Priya Abraham, "Let My People Go," *World Magazine*, February 24, 2007. Reproduced by permission.

the Slaves, a slave in the American South in 1850 cost $40,000 in today's dollars. Today, the average cost of a slave is $90. A growing world population with millions of poor means an ample supply of potential slaves that has driven down the price.

That means slaveholders may not need to keep slaves as a long-term, generational investment: If a slave falls ill or otherwise cannot work, he or she is easy to replace.

What does slavery in 2007 look like? Chattel slavery is now relatively rare, largely limited to parts of Africa. Most of today's slaves—about 20 million—are in debt bondage, and mostly in the South Asian countries of India, Pakistan, and Nepal. Others in places such as Southeast Asia and Brazil are contract laborers, lured by promises of well-paying jobs but forced to remain in harsh, menial conditions. Forced marriages enslave women and girls. Human trafficking, which ensnares 600,000 to 800,000 people a year, is the newest slave trade and the world's third-largest criminal business after drugs and arms dealing.

Bonded slavery works this way: A poor man takes a loan to pay for an emergency such as a funeral or family illness. He repays it with his labor, although unscrupulous lenders will not say for how long. Soon, as the original debt does not diminish, he realizes the lender has trapped him—and often his family—into working years or generations without pay.

A Tough Fight

Nagaraj was such a man. Desperate for work, he took a loan from a brick kiln owner who also bonded his wife and children. Nagaraj was devastated: At 12, he had worked with his parents for three years to pay off a debt, and now his family was in the same predicament.

Like his fellow slaves, Nagaraj and his family lived in a concrete cell at the brick factory. Six days a week, his family began work at 1 a.m., slogging 16 hours and working under the hot sun. He said he hated seeing his children work as hard as the adults and fall ill, growing up as another man's property. If workers complained or bolted, the kiln owner beat them savagely.

In 2004, the Virginia-based International Justice Mission (IJM) worked with local authorities to raid the kiln, freeing 138 people, including Nagaraj and his family. The kiln owner faces prosecution, while Nagaraj and his wife now run their own brick-making business and send their children to school.

Freeing slaves is one hurdle abolitionists have to clear, but keeping them free is another.

Nagaraj's case is the kind IJM's workers see often in South Asia. As modern-day abolitionists, IJM hires lawyers and human-rights advocates to fill a crucial if ironic niche in fighting slavery: They work to ensure local officials enforce laws.

Despite ample laws at the local, national, and international level against bonded labor and other forms of slavery, each case involves a long and hard fight. Where police and authorities are corrupt, they let the powerful prey on the poor, says IJM senior vice president of interventions, Sharon Cohn: "If a young girl in a poor community is a victim of sexual assault, the rapist often has better connections with the police than the family will," she told *World.*

In slave terms, if people come cheap, she says, then slaveholders should pay dearly in other ways—with jail time. Cohn says it takes grit and tenacity to pursue such prosecutions, where bonded labor easily blurs into sex trafficking. In IJM's biggest success, staff and Cambodian police raided brothels in Svay Pak. They rescued little girls between the ages of 5 and 10. The pedophiles caught running the brothels have received prison sentences.

Child Labor Is Severely Overlooked

Freeing slaves is one hurdle abolitionists have to clear, but keeping them free is another. Sivakasi is a city in India's southeastern state of Tamil Nadu, dubbed "Little Japan" for its matchstick, fireworks, and printing industries. Behind factory doors, however, are thousands of bonded child workers, making the city one of India's worst slavery hubs.

Most of India's bonded slaves are "untouchables"—Hinduism's outcasts now more charitably known as Dalits, or the "downtrodden." Dalits are desperately poor, and so most at risk for becoming enslaved.

The Dalit Freedom Network (DFN), an advocacy and charitable group, helps run a network of schools for Dalit children and, in Sivakasi, the students come from surrounding cottage factories.

They come, but not always regularly. Twelve-year-old Manjula is one such student. At first, her parents often pulled her from school to work in the factory, desperate for the extra cents a day she earned. Manjula began working with her parents at their local matchstick factory when she was 4.

The adults usually prepare the dangerous chemicals for the match heads—chlorates, phosphorus, and sulphur—and cut the sticks to size. The children work separately, typically in a 300-square-foot workroom lit dimly by a small, high window. The only ventilation is a concrete grille in the wall.

Though owners bribe local police to look away, the window's strategic placement prevents passersby from looking in, since India bans children under 14 from working. The children sit in rows, peering at their matchsticks. They dip each in sulfur, lay it to dry—often on a newspaper—then place it in a match box. Dip, dry, dip, dry, goes the work, for 12 hours or more at a stretch. If the children meet the quota, they get less than $1. More reliably, they get chronic bronchitis and allergic skin rashes.

Manjula worked seven years in a matchstick factory and now labors to breathe sometimes. The school's teachers cajoled her parents to let her stay in school, though her younger sister still has to work. Manjula had to start at kindergarten level, having never learned the alphabet or how to count.

Hopes for the Future

When students like her miss class, teachers visit their parents and coax them into returning. More students skip school during the seasonal Hindu festivals, when demand for fireworks and matches is high. Sivakasi supplies three-quarters of India's matches and almost all its fireworks.

Persuasion on the benefits of education doesn't always work, said Albert Lael, national director of Dalit education for Operation Mercy Charitable Company, a partner with DFN. "The problem is [families] want their immediate needs met," he said. "[There's] a long way to go because they don't see the benefit they get in the long run." Many Dalits have been slaves so long, they think only like slaves. Ask them what they want to do with their future, and they often name menial jobs.

Lael has loftier hopes. A Dalit himself, he sees the children and remembers his grandfather's plight "was exactly like the kids in Sivakasi." Canadian missionaries educated his family, and Lael now holds an MBA [master's degree in business administration]. But pulling other Dalits alongside him can be hard labor with few compensations, too.

DFN schools know to compromise. The parents of one student, 11-year-old Shiva, let him attend for seven years only because he also continues to work. So when school is out at 3 p.m., he dips and packs matches for another 12 hours. Exhausted, he struggles to do his homework and keep up. But school is a haven: fresh air and playtime, sports and lessons.

Cultural Limitations for Women

For years Afghan women have suffered under a slave system actually sanctioned in customary law called baad. Under baad, a family offers a daughter in marriage as a debt payment or as restitution for a crime. Womankind, a British nonprofit, reported [in 2006] that between 60 percent and 80 percent of Afghan marriages are forced. More than half of Afghan women marry before age 16, and some as young as 6.

Modern-day abolitionists admit they can free only so many slaves at a time from such conditions.

Two seasons of drought and a bad winter mean Afghan families have turned more desperate, with reports of some selling their daughters to feed their other children. In Helmand Province, which produces most of Afghanistan's opium crop, some farmers cannot repay drug smugglers for loans to plant opium. So they turn to trading in women instead. [In 2006], the UN reports, a 25-year-old woman who had been traded for an opium debt turned an AK-47 [rifle] on herself after suffering daily beatings from her husband.

Other bonded women who commit suicide, however, set themselves on fire. Medica Mondiale, a German group that helps women in conflict zones, found hundreds of cases of self-immolation in Afghanistan. Among some survivors, the group's workers found women lying in hospital scarred and screaming with pain.

Medica Mondiale project manager Ancil Adrian-Paul lived in Afghanistan [in 2006] and recounted one case: A 17-year-old girl survived self-immolation after her father married her to a man in Iran who beat her. Once a girl marries, she leaves her family. The saying goes, "The only way you come back is in a white coffin."

Desperate, the girl said a voice repeated to her, "Burn yourself, burn yourself." When she awoke, she could not remember if the burning had been deliberate or accidental. The girl needs six more operations to repair her ravaged body, but she was speaking publicly about her experience.

Modern-day abolitionists admit they can free only so many slaves at a time from such conditions. Groups like IJM asked *World* that specific locations of their work not be disclosed, lest the reports jeopardize their workers. And slave victims, including those in this story, use aliases to protect their families and their own lives from retribution at the hands of contemporary slave traders.

Twenty-first-century slavery may stretch in directions Wilberforce never imagined, but its crucial trait has not changed: One person still controls another completely, using coercion, force, and restrictions on all movement. Like Wilberforce, abolitionists today have a keen eye for freedom—and they see plenty of work left to do.

CHAPTER 3

Can Global Cooperation Reduce Human Trafficking?

Chapter Preface

As part of its continued efforts to eradicate human trafficking worldwide, the U.S. government launched the International Violence Against Women Act (I-VAWA) in 2007. Building on the Violence Against Women Act of 1994, then–U.S. senator Joe Biden proposed that the act extend beyond U.S. borders in an effort to stop violence against women around the globe, specifically targeting the ten to fifteen countries in which women are most victimized. The act also would provide more than a billion dollars in support to foreign nongovernmental organizations (NGOs) to aid their efforts to combat the abuse and trafficking of women and girls. Although the I-VAWA received tremendous support from government agencies and NGOs worldwide, its controversial nature resulted in defeat in both the Senate and the House. Nonetheless, organizations continue to fight for its passage.

Organizations that support the I-VAWA argue that it would make fighting violence against women a U.S. diplomatic policy for the first time in history. More specifically, it would work to end the rape and enslavement of women and girls in wartorn countries by giving the U.S. military the right to protect them and to prosecute their aggressors. According to U.S.-based Women Thrive Worldwide, the I-VAWA is supported by and was drafted in consultation with nearly two hundred government and NGO groups worldwide, including the Family Violence Prevention Fund. In a supporting statement on its Web site, Amnesty International USA argues that "violence against women and girls is one of the underlying factors that contributes to a person's vulnerability to being trafficked, and many women face violence as they are trafficked." The I-VAWA will allow for provisions to stop these acts.

Not everyone supports the passage of the I-VAWA. Conservative columnist Phyllis Schlafly responded to the act in a

Feburary 2007 article in *Human Events* in which she claims that passage of the I-VAWA not only would not help women in other lands, it also would worsen matters for American women. She argues that the push to pass the act is merely an effort by feminist groups lobbying for the U.S. government to ratify the United Nations' Convention on the Elimination of All Forms of Discrimination Against Women, which she believes is corrupt. She cites examples of abuse against women from many of the signing countries as proof that such actions are not effective. She concludes, "The International Violence Against Women Act is based on the lie that violence against women is the same problem in all countries. Many non-Western countries have social norms that justify abuse (such as genital mutilation, forced marriage, and polygamy), and 'international standards' would vastly diminish the rights and benefits U.S. women now enjoy."

Although the I-VAWA may never be passed, the international community will persist in seeking the means to stop violence against women and to put an end to human trafficking. After all, as a report by Women Thrive Worldwide demonstrates, "at least one out of every three women worldwide are beaten, coerced into sex, or otherwise abused in her lifetime, with rates reaching 70% in some countries." The authors in this chapter debate the effectiveness of global cooperation in this fight.

Educating International Military Forces Can Reduce Human Trafficking

Keith J. Allred

Keith J. Allred is professor of law at the George C. Marshall European Center for Security Studies in Garmisch-Partenkirchen, Germany, and holds the rank of captain in the Judge Advocate General's Corps of the U.S. Navy.

Over 140 years after slavery was outlawed in the United States, and nearly eighty years after world leaders signed the Slavery Convention, human slavery and enforced servitude continue to doom millions to lives of involuntary servitude in our day. The U.S. State Department's 2005 Report on Human Trafficking estimates that 600,000–800,000 persons are trafficked across international borders every year. Many more, perhaps millions, are trafficked within the borders of their own nations. The International Labor Organization estimates that there are about 12.3 million people enslaved in various kinds of forced or bonded labor, sexual or involuntary servitude at any given time. Some are kidnapped, while others are enticed by promises of good jobs abroad. Some are sold to traffickers by their parents or husbands; many simply migrate of their own accord in search of work, and find themselves in the hands of traffickers. Like the slaves of times past, many labor in fields and factories, yet a more pernicious form of human bondage has become the most common form of servitude: sexual slavery. . . .

Ironically, there continues to be a demand for cheap crops harvested by trafficked farm workers, cheap textile products

Keith J. Allred, "Human Trafficking: Breaking the Military Link," *Connections: PfP Consortium Quarterly Journal*, Winter 2005, pp. 63–72. Copyright © 2005 Partnership for Peace Consortium of Defense Academies and Security Institutes (PfP Consortium). Reproduced by permission.

produced by trafficked garment workers, and cheap sexual services provided by trafficked sex workers. While on one level society recoils at human trafficking and strives to destroy it, on another level society provides the demand, knowingly or not, for the cheap goods and services that trafficked persons provide. Yet in recent years the scourge of human trafficking has come increasingly before the public eye. Governments and international organizations have begun to recognize trafficking as a growing and pernicious evil. As it has come to be seen as a source of funding for crime and terror, governments and other organizations have begun to attack the factors that support it. This article will address only one aspect of the problem of human trafficking: the role of military personnel in creating demand for trafficked persons. Both the United States Army and UN peacekeeping forces have recently experienced embarrassments suggesting an unacceptable relationship between trafficked women and their soldiers abroad. The reactions of both organizations to these revelations have been both positive and strong. NATO [North Atlantic Treaty Organization], another significant source of troops deployed around the world, has joined the effort in a similar way. There is reason to hope that the combined initiatives of these three military forces will do much to reduce the demand for trafficked women and to increase the pressure placed on those who make commerce of trafficked persons. While the "war" on human trafficking must be fought on several fronts—including prevention, prosecution, and protection, and including enslaved individuals ranging from sweatshop and agricultural workers to child soldiers, and even camel jockeys—there are movements afoot that hold the promise of removing deployed military personnel as a significant factor in the demand for trafficked women.

U.S. Troops and International Prostitution

Military personnel deployed away from their homes have been a long-standing source of demand for sexual services from local populations. During the Vietnam years, United States military personnel inspected and certified local prostitutes for service in Thailand, Vietnam, and the Philippines, and organized "Rest and Recreation" facilities for U.S. troops that included easy access to prostitutes. In some cases, an overly close proximity between U.S. troops and brothels has exposed the Army to allegations that it was essentially operating its own military houses of prostitution. Today, the United States has nearly 250,000 members of its military forces deployed in combat and peacekeeping operations around the world. If the number of troops normally resident abroad is added to this total, there are nearly 350,000 Americans stationed in nearly 130 countries around the world. These sheer numbers may tend to make deployed U.S. military personnel one of the largest sources of demand for sexual services around the world, some of which would likely be provided by trafficked women. And yet the United States Army has begun to take steps to ensure that its troops do not contribute to this demand.

The Defense Department established a "zero-tolerance" policy, which prohibited U.S. troops and the contractors who support them from being "complicit in any way in the trafficking in persons."

In May of 2002, Fox News broadcast a story suggesting that U.S. Army patrols of the red light districts in Korea were actually providing protection to establishments where trafficked women were "employed." The suggestion that the U.S. Army was involved in facilitating the trafficking of sexual slaves was unmistakable, and provoked a strong reaction in Congress. Thirteen U.S. Congressmen asked the Inspector General (IG) of the Department of Defense to organize a thorough and comprehensive investigation into the relationship between U.S. armed forces and prostitution, including the prostitution of trafficked women. The IG responded quickly, with separate investigations into Korea and the Balkans. These reports, issued in July and December of 2003, did not find that U.S. troops were protecting the brothels or facilitating the trafficking of persons, but did agree that the Army's relationship with those establishments was "overly familiar" and that concerns about human trafficking had been overlooked. But the report also determined that many of the women working in those establishments had been trafficked, and that they had suffered such offenses as confiscation of personal identity papers and physical violence.

The U.S. Government Takes Action

Even the Inspector General's conclusion of an "overly familiar" relationship between human traffickers and the U.S. armed forces resulted in a pronounced response. The Defense Department established a "zero-tolerance" policy, which prohibited U.S. troops and the contractors who support them from being "complicit in any way in the trafficking in persons." The policy defines trafficking to include involuntary servitude and debt bondage, as well as sexual slavery. The commander of the U.S. forces in Korea also responded to the investigation with an expansion of the use of "off-limits" areas, prohibiting U.S. personnel from patronizing establishments that had been placed "off-limits" for suspected involvement in human trafficking. Military patrols of off-limits areas are now clearly instructed to prevent U.S. personnel from patronizing these establishments, and the appearance of U.S. forces providing protection for them is no longer remotely acceptable.

The zero-tolerance policy and expanded use of off-limits areas has been combined with an expanded education campaign for all U.S. troops reporting for duty in Korea. In testimony before the House Armed Services Committee given on 21 September 2003, General Leon LaPorte noted that all new arrivals, including U.S. Navy ships visiting Korean ports, are exposed to counter-trafficking training that alerts troops and sailors to the issue of trafficking, identifies off-limits areas, emphasizes the zero-tolerance policy, and describes potential disciplinary measures for violations. Other initiatives to reduce U.S. troops' patronage of establishments that may be involved in human trafficking include expanded recreational activities for military personnel on base; expanded cultural, service, and educational opportunities both on and off-base; a 24-hour hotline where military personnel can report businesses suspected of trafficking; self-produced TV advertisements seen by both U.S. and Korean populations that discuss the issue of trafficking; and a "Prostitution and Human Trafficking Identification Guidebook" that helps military personnel identify and avoid establishments that appear to be engaged in human trafficking. Courtesy patrols and undercover operations in areas where trafficking may be occurring further monitor the presence of U.S. personnel in these areas and discourage their patronage of prostitutes.

Incidents of sexual assault perpetrated by UN peacekeepers have been documented in Angola, Cambodia, East Timor, Liberia, Mozambique, Kosovo, Sierra Leone, and Somalia.

Criminalizing Soldiers' Solicitation

The Army's embarrassed reaction to human trafficking in Korea may also have been on President [George W.] Bush's mind when he addressed the United Nations General Assembly on 23 September 2003. He identified human trafficking as a "special evil" that merited the UN's attention, devoting a substantial portion of his remarks to the topic. In February 2004, the President issued Executive Order 13257 establishing a task force to combat human trafficking. Later that month he issued a National Security Presidential Directive on trafficking that gave additional emphasis to the army's initiatives.

In another remarkable innovation, on 15 September 2004 the Department of Defense's Joint Service Committee on Military Justice proposed several changes to the Uniform Code of

Military Justice (UCMJ), a federal criminal code that applies to active duty military personnel worldwide, at all hours of the day, regardless of their deployment status. Under the UCMJ, U.S. military personnel can be tried for military offenses such as disrespect and failure to obey orders, as well as the more traditional criminal offenses. Among the proposals was a suggested new criminal offense of "patronizing a prostitute," intended to completely eliminate U.S. forces from the equation of demand for paid sexual services anywhere worldwide. Under the proposed legislation, patronizing a prostitute would become a crime for all military personnel after 1 July 2005. The new offense would punish the soldier-customer even if the sex act is consensual and prostitution is legal in the country where the act occurs.

NATO's and the United Nations' Efforts

NATO has taken similar steps intended to remove its troops from proximity to, or an "overly familiar" relationship with, human trafficking, particularly for purposes of sexual slavery. In July 2003, the issue of NATO involvement in human trafficking appears to have been first raised by then-U.S. Ambassador to Moldova Pamela Smith, who indicated that peacekeepers stationed in the country created demand for prostitutes, which translated into demand for trafficked women. In March 2004, the U.S. and Norwegian Ambassadors to NATO, Nicholas Burns and Kai Eide, hosted the organization's first conference to address the problem of human trafficking, and to consider whether NATO personnel posted abroad were contributing to the demand. By June of that year, NATO had developed a draft "Policy on Combating Trafficking in Human Beings" that received the endorsement of NATO heads of state and governments. The NATO policy calls upon all NATO member states (and all non-NATO states that contribute troops or civilian personnel to NATO missions) to do all that they can to ensure that their troops do not contribute to or support trafficking in persons in any way. The key language of the policy prohibits NATO forces, contractors, and employees conducting operations under NATO command and control from "engaging in trafficking in human beings or facilitating it." Like the U.S. response in Korea, NATO sees training and education programs as being essential to reducing the engagement of prostitutes by NATO forces deployed abroad on NATO missions. Appendix II to the NATO policy outlines specific requirements of such training programs, including pre-deployment training for all, and special training for commanders and for military police units. The policy's prohibition also applies to any civilian element accompanying such forces, including contractors.

The Fox News report that caused such a reaction in the United States Army in Korea only hinted at official involvement in human trafficking. By contrast, the UN has been buffeted by allegations of serious sexual misconduct by its peacekeepers in many parts of the world for many years. Incidents of sexual assault perpetrated by UN peacekeepers have been documented in Angola, Cambodia, East Timor, Liberia, Mozambique, Kosovo, Sierra Leone, and Somalia. When UN peacekeepers deployed to Bosnia-Herzegovina, brothels containing trafficked women developed quickly in the areas surrounding UN compounds. Former Human Rights Watch researcher Martina Vandenberg wrote, "Brothels sprouted like mushrooms, surrounding the base on all sides." The UN suffered not only by the clear proximal association of prostitution and its troops, but by testimony regarding sexual offenses by its troops, and by testimony offered before a committee of the U.S. House of Representatives that high-level UN officials had attempted to conceal the offenses. UN personnel also took with them hundreds of files regarding human trafficking when the UN mission in Bosnia turned over its duties to the European Union Police Mission at the end of 2002. This prevented evidence regarding trafficking that may have been embarrassing to the UN from falling into EU [European Union] hands. At the very least, it represented an absolute failure of cooperation in the turnover.

UN Peacekeepers Enable Organized Crime

These signal embarrassments were revived, if not eclipsed, in the spring of 2004 when allegations of peacekeeper misconduct surfaced in the Congo. Complaints that UN peacekeepers had committed sixty-eight instances of rape, pedophilia, and prostitution upon the Congolese people were bad enough, but they were aggravated by reports of peacekeepers interfering with the investigation, paying or offering to pay witnesses to change their testimony, threatening investigators, and refusing to identify colleagues who were suspected of offenses. Later research has concluded that up to 90 percent of the women engaging in normal prostitution in the Balkans were victims of human trafficking. As a result, not only were the peacekeepers engaged in rape and pedophilia, they were, perhaps unknowingly, supporting the trade in trafficked women and feeding the coffers of organized crime. Counter-trafficking expert and former U.K. [United Kingdom] police inspector Paul Holmes indicates that peacekeepers who exploit trafficked women "unwittingly support precisely the people who do not want a safe, stable, and secure environment"—i.e., organized criminals.

The Secretary-General of the UN was understandably outraged to learn that UN troops had committed these offenses while serving under the peacekeeping banner, but at the same time he could not have been surprised. He sent Jordanian Prince Zeid Ra'ad Zeid Al-Hussein to the Congo to investigate the allegations, and confirmed that they were true. The prince's report was released to the public in March 2005, featuring an objective report of the problem and its causes, as well as an outline of steps the UN and its member nations can take now to reduce or control it. The UN has thus found itself fairly in the limelight, with the opportunity to join the U.S. Army and NATO in seeking ways to prevent its troops from supporting trafficking or engaging in sexual misconduct while deployed on missions. The examples already set by the U.S. Army and NATO may well have informed and assisted development of the report's recommendations. . . .

The connection between trafficking and organized crime . . . may add muscle to the effort to crack down on both peacekeepers and prostitutes.

With the UN's history of peacekeeper abuses, obstruction of investigations, removal of evidence, its lack of common disciplinary authority, and an apparent organizational climate of cover up and obfuscation, it may well be that the report's recommendations will amount to nothing. So far, repatriation seems to be the only result that befalls any peacekeeper accused of crime. Even the prince's report admits that the perception that peacekeepers are never prosecuted for crimes that they commit while deployed overseas is "justified."

Hope for the Future

And yet there is room to be cautiously optimistic. The UN's humiliation comes at a time when other major military forces are also beginning to grapple with the connection between armed forces and trafficked women who are forced into prostitution. The connection between trafficking and organized crime, which threatens the security that peacekeepers are trying to establish, may add muscle to the effort to crack down on both peacekeepers and prostitutes. The knowledge that the proceeds of human trafficking are funding organized crime and terrorist operations may actually give national commanders the determination to make things different when the UN sends peacekeepers to the field. If this can be done—carefully, and without offending any Troop Contributing Nation—the results could significantly reduce the demand for trafficked women that UN Peacekeepers currently represent.

Human trafficking is one of the great scourges of our day, and is doubly damned because it feeds both organized crime and terrorist organizations. After a long slumber, nations of the world have begun to awaken and take firm and resolute action against both the demand and the supply sides of the equation. The role of military forces deployed abroad has come to be seen as a strong component of the demand for trafficked women, which in today's world is increasingly unacceptable to modern governments and the international organizations in which they participate. It is perhaps fortunate that the United States and United Nations have both suffered embarrassing revelations about the demand their deployed troops create for trafficked persons, particularly prostitutes. Whether mutually or independently, each has reached the conclusion that they must ensure that their military personnel must not be complicit in, or facilitate in any way, the trade in trafficked persons.

The steps taken by the U.S. and NATO (and those recommended for the UN) are clearly a step in the right direction, but how large a step remains to be seen. The task is not merely to give a brief training presentation before NATO troops deploy. It is to change the mindset of a whole society to the point where soldiers of every stripe actually see prostitution for what it is: a modern slave trade that fuels crime and instability and funds international terrorism. With strong leadership, disciplinary consequences that are real and significant, and other alternatives for off-duty recreation, there is a real possibility that deployed military personnel will diminish the role that they play in the demand for trafficked women. This in turn could do much to reduce the victimization of trafficked women and the evils that flow from this contemporary slave trade.

Efforts Against Human Trafficking in the United States Extend Worldwide

Tara McKelvey

Tara McKelvey is a senior editor at the American Prospect *and the author of* Monstering: Inside America's Policy on Secret Interrogations and Torture in the Terror War.

Sharon Cohn stops for a moment to adjust the screen before hitting the "play" button on the VCR in her office. Cohn works for a human rights organization called International Justice Mission [IJM], based in Arlington, Virginia. On the screen is a five-minute montage of scenes shot over a three-week period from January to February 2003 in Svay Pak, Cambodia, a booming red-light district just outside [the capital city of] Phnom Penh.

In one scene, American sex tourists stroll along a bustling street past a bar called Home Away from Home, and local pimps approach them. In another, a girl with longish bangs and huge dark eyes is standing in a room. She doesn't know it, but shes being filmed by an I.J.M. investigator with an undercover camera.

"How old?" he asks.

"Ten," she says, smiling. The film breaks off, and another girl, who also says she's 10, appears. Her hair is pulled back by a plastic, heart-shaped barrette. These girls, Cohn explains, are being sold to tourists for sex.

On March 29, 2003, I.J.M. staff members and Cambodian law-enforcement officers raided some of the brothels shown in the film. The following October, six people were convicted on trafficking-related offenses and sentenced to 5 to 15 years in prison. Three months later, in January, one brothel-keeper was sentenced to 20 years.

"The trials in Cambodia were by far the most satisfying trial experience I've had," says Cohn, 33, who worked as a corporate lawyer for a Washington firm, Arnold & Porter, before joining I.J.M. to head its intervention efforts.

Over the past several years, Cohn and her colleagues have conducted such raids and various types of rescue missions in Latin America, South Asia, Southeast Asia and Africa. [As of] 2004, I.J.M. [had] helped more than 150 victims of child sexual exploitation or trafficking. Local government agencies and nongovernmental organizations provide care for the children after they have been rescued, and Cohn likes to keep in touch with them. She reads aloud from a letter:

"How are you? I'm well. Please don't worry about me. Now I'm studying sewing and cross stitch. Thanks for the sweets. They were yummy."

Combating a Growing Problem

According to a U.S. State Department report, *Trafficking in Persons*, released [in] June [2004], 600,000 to 800,000 people are trafficked across international borders each year. Approximately 70 percent are women and half of them are children. The majority of women and girls are victims of the commercial sex trade.

The [George W.] Bush administration devoted nearly $74 million to anti-trafficking activities worldwide in fiscal year 2003, according to the State Department. As one of the leading faith-based organizations involved in the anti-trafficking programs, I.J.M. was praised by federal officials at a February 2003 conference, "Pathbreaking Strategies in the Global Fight Against Sex Trafficking," and it has received money from the U.S. Agency for International Development for its work in Cambodia. I.J.M. was also cited in a June 8, 2004, *New York*

Times article about Americans who commit sex crimes overseas and the U.S. government's recently expanded efforts to prosecute them in this country.

In the early 1990's, I.J.M.'s founder and president, Gary Haugen, 41, worked as counsel in the civil rights division of the U.S. Justice Department; then, in 1994, he became officer in charge of the United Nation's investigation of genocide in Rwanda. The idea behind I.J.M., which opened its doors in April 1997, emerged from his experience during those years. He decided to create a way to address the suffering and injustice that staff of faith-based private aid agencies saw in other countries—but were powerless to stop. Indeed, says Haugen, many of them seemed paralyzed by despair. His approach in I.J.M., then, was to take on oppression step by step.

Trafficking prospers in places where criminals can profit from the enterprise because laws against it are not strictly enforced.

Aid workers often "observe severe human rights abuses in the communities where they serve," he explained to the House Subcommittee on International Terrorism, Nonproliferation and Human Rights on June 25, 2003. "These workers refer these cases to us, and then we conduct a professional investigation to document the abuses and mobilize intervention on behalf of the victims."

Today a staff of lawyers, criminal investigators and government-relations experts work out of the Washington office, in eight field offices in countries such as Thailand and the Philippines and in recently opened offices in Cambodia, Zambia and Uganda. I.J.M. staff work on a range of human rights issues, including efforts to free victims of bonded slavery in South Asia; protect the legal rights of African widows whose husbands die of AIDS (many lose their land after the deaths of their husbands); prosecute rape cases in Peru; and defend children who have been imprisoned for petty crimes in the Philippines.

Subverting the Law

Haugen's background in law enforcement guides I.J.M.'s approach to addressing human rights abuses. For example, he explains, trafficking prospers in places where criminals can profit from the enterprise because laws against it are not strictly enforced. Therefore, I.J.M. works closely with local police on a variety of cases, helping officers develop investigative leads and collect evidence.

"If the customers can find the victims of sex trafficking whenever they want, so can the police," Haugen told the House subcommittee. "How, therefore, do you possibly get away with running a sex trafficking enterprise? You do so only if permitted by local law enforcement."

Sex trafficking and commercial sexual exploitation can be drastically reduced wherever a country has the political will and the operational capacity to send the perpetrators to jail.

Haugen says he believes people of faith have an obligation to help those who are suffering or oppressed. "When our grandchildren ask us where we were when the weak, the helpless and the vulnerable of our era needed people of compassion and purpose and hope," says Haugen, "I hope we can say that we showed up—and that we showed up on time."

In early 2003, correspondents from television's *Dateline NBC* program accompanied Cambodian police and I.J.M. staff on a raid of Cambodian brothels as they removed the children from the premises and helped place as many as possible in safe houses. Footage of the raid aired in a Jan. 23 segment titled "Children for Sale."

Shortly after the segment appeared on TV, a 54-year-old radiologist from Tulsa, Oklahoma, who was secretly recorded by *Dateline* producers as he talked about paying for sex with underaged girls, was placed under investigation by the Oklahoma state medical licensure board. I.J.M. turned its evidence over to the U.S. Department of Justice and has cooperated with law enforcement agencies around the world that are prosecuting Western sex tourists.

Beyond Raids and Trials

But critics of I.J.M.'s approach argue that the group's emphasis on criminal justice addresses only part of the problem. "The argument has been made that you can't effectively combat trafficking unless you attack poverty," says Cohn. "It simply isn't true. We have been in places in East Africa where there's poverty, but we weren't able to find kids for sale. It happens in an environment that tolerates it and where there is no local law enforcement."

That's why I.J.M. staffers are trying to assist local officials—by helping to collect statements from witnesses and providing copies of videos made during their own investigations. They also give prosecutors testimony their investigators have gathered. As a result of such cooperation, countries such as Cambodia have invited I.J.M. to train their local law enforcement officers. Most recently, the government of Bolivia has asked I.J.M. to train police officers in the humane treatment of street children.

After children—and women—are saved from brothels, I.J.M. staffers help them settle into programs sponsored by "local aftercare partners," says Penny Hunter, I.J.M.'s vice president of communications. The programs are designed "to ensure that a safe and nurturing home is provided for rescued victims," she adds. Finally, I.J.M caseworkers follow up with the victims to help ease their transition to a new life.

Haugen sums up the struggle: "Sex trafficking and commercial sexual exploitation can be drastically reduced wherever a country has the political will and the operational capacity to send the perpetrators to jail and to treat the victims with compassion and dignity. This is a fight that can actually be won."

Global Efforts Can Reduce Human Trafficking in the Persian Gulf States

Barbara Degorge

Barbara Degorge is a professor at the American University in Dubai, United Arab Emirates.

It is a simple and accepted truth that slavery exists in the twenty-first century. More and more, people are becoming aware that this practice persists, as much or more so than it did 100 years ago. Contemporary slavery is not a phenomenon of modernity, rather it is a timeless institution that has continued to evolve. Today more than 27 million people are enslaved worldwide, ranging from the African continent, Europe, North and South America to the Middle East. Moreover, the type of slavery and the conditions under which it exists have changed due to increased globalization and modernization.

In the last few years the case of Sudan has brought slavery to public attention with the news about the civil war between the North and South revealing a bustling market in human trafficking. However, other regions where slavery is practiced receive little or no attention. One of these regions is the Arabian Gulf which has altogether escaped world attention. This lack of attention is mainly explained by the rapid modernization and development of the Gulf States, where modern skyscrapers and advanced technology hide grimmer realities. This paper examines the different forms of slavery practiced daily in one of the Gulf States—the United Arab Emirates [UAE]. . . .

In the Middle East and especially in the Gulf States there is today an active slave trade. Three types of slavery are prac-

Barbara Degorge, "Modern Day Slavery in the United Arab Emirates," *The European Legacy*, vol. 11, October 2006, pp. 657–665. Copyright © 2006 Taylor & Francis Group, LLC. Reproduced by permission of Taylor & Francis, Ltd., http//:www.tandf.co.uk/journals and the author.

ticed: exploitation of children, chattel slavery, and "migrant worker" slavery, people who arrive of their own free will with the intention of bettering their lot. These migrants, however, do not always know what they are getting into or how to deal with the situations they fall prey to. This tripartite classification of slavery is close to the UN definition of serfdom; however, the latter term is misleading as the slave is not tied to the land; it applies insofar as both cases entail the slave's total lack of mobility.

Exploitation of children is probably the most shocking form of slavery the world has witnessed in recent times. It is practiced not only in the United Arab Emirates but in India and many Asian countries. The UAE exploits children mainly as camel jockeys. Children as young as three-year-olds are used to ride camels because of their small size and weight. They are tied to the camel's back so that they won't fall off, which enables the camel to race without the encumbrance of an adult person. As in most countries, slavery in the UAE was outlawed (in 2003): it is illegal for a child under 15 years or weighing less than 45 kilos [99 lbs] to be a camel jockey. However, the oil rich countries of the Gulf region find it more profitable to continue this centuries-old practice of buying children from the Indian subcontinent—India, Bangladesh, Pakistan—as well as from Sudan. Many are kidnapped; many are sold into slavery because their families are too poor to support them. It is estimated that as many as 5,000 children, from two years and upwards, have been kidnapped or bought to be used as camel jockeys. Being a camel jockey is a seven-day-a-week job, all year round—even in times of extreme heat, which most people in the Gulf States would strive to avoid. The children are maltreated: they are woken up in the middle of the night to clean camel dung with their bare hands; they are beaten if they do not perform well enough and many are injured, killed or maimed during the camel races; they receive no schooling; have no idea about their family origins and are regularly beaten to keep them in line. Some are sexually molested by the trainers, as Peter Conradi reports. When children grow too old or physically big to be camel jockeys, they are lucky if they find employment in one of the camel stables or else are simply left to fend for themselves. This is an extremely dangerous situation for youngsters as throughout the Middle East it is illegal not to hold legal residency status, thus making them subject to fines or incarceration.

In 2004, a Pakistani human rights attorney, Ansar Burney, finally succeeded in bringing the problem of child slavery to public attention in the UAE. After spending two weeks filming this form of slavery in action, Burney convinced Sheikh Mohammed bin Rashid al Nahyan of Abu Dhabi to see the film. The film exposed the bare facts of the trade and all who viewed it were horrified. In March 2005, the Emirati Sheikhs pledged that they were going to put a stop to the practice, which had become a cause of embarrassment for the wealthy Gulf States. They set up "refugee" homes for the boys while an attempt was made to find their families. However, many were too young when they became slaves even to remember who they were or where they came from, which is why so many of them are still in the UAE. Although the practice was outlawed again in 2005, this does not mean that it no longer exists. Human rights groups such as Anti-Slavery International are concerned that it will not really be banned given that a similar law was initiated in 2002. This form of human trafficking, the only way to classify this practice, thus continues throughout the Gulf States.

Another form of human trafficking that is prevalent in the Gulf States, specifically in the UAE, Saudi Arabia, Kuwait, and Qatar, is the forcing of women and children into the sex trade. Saul Hudson points out that the United States has criticized these four Arab countries as the worst offenders in the human sex trade, but the offenders have done virtually nothing to stop the practice of women being used as sex slaves.

Many of the women who enter into this type of slavery do so without knowing what they are getting into. They come to the Gulf States with the idea of starting a new life and finding a job in order to help their families in their home country. They leave their homes, come to the UAE, Kuwait, or another Gulf country, arriving in the home of an Arab family to work as maids or child carers. One such woman, Kamala Rai, arrived in Saudi Arabia in the hope of opening a shop. Instead, her sponsor locked her up, beat her and raped her. The journals she wrote, later found in her suitcase when she finally returned to her native Nepal, illustrate the horrors she experienced during her three-and-a-half-month stay in the Gulf. Others are kept in prostitution homes where they are forced to serve any customer at any time of the day or night.

In 2005 the US State Department cited the case of a young Uzbekistani orphan girl who was sold into slavery in the UAE. She was kept as a prostitute until deemed "unusable." At this point, as Hudson reports, the UAE immigration service stepped in and declared her an illegal immigrant, for which offence she was sentenced to two years in prison.

As one walks down the streets of Dubai, the most liberal of the Emirates, or goes into one of its many hotels, one sees many prostitutes from Eastern Europe. But Dubai is not the only Emirate where prostitution is visible; it is seen in all the Emirates as well as the neighboring Gulf States. Many of these women, from Southeast Asia or Eastern Europe, whether sold as prostitutes or arriving with the expectation of finding respectable employment, find themselves trapped. They are unable to free themselves because, overwhelmed by shame they fear to tell anyone back home what has befallen them.

The two forms of slavery discussed above are practiced not only in the Gulf but worldwide. The sex trade thrives in New York and Paris. The camel jockey, although unique to the Gulf, is only one form of child slave labor, which exists in other forms throughout the world.

The third type of slavery in the Gulf region is that of migrant workers. A migrant worker is someone who has come from another place to perform a job on a temporary basis. About 75% of the population of the UAE can be classified as migrant workers, though most would prefer to be defined as "expatriates." They are certainly expatriates but they are all also migrant workers. They may be divided into two groups: those who have well paid jobs and those who work for next to nothing. But can this be defined as slavery, for, after all, it is directly tied to earning wages? It also raises the question asked earlier: what is it that makes a person free? There is no set definition of wage slavery, only differing views. . . .

Slavery today is voluntary: willingly but perhaps unknowingly people give up their freedoms.

In the Gulf States there is an inordinate number of foreign workers dispersed throughout the region. In the UAE, 90% of the workforce is not Emirati. Out of a population of approximately 2.8 million, it is estimated that 1.5 million people come from the Indian subcontinent with the balance of foreigners from western countries and southeast Asia. This is an astronomical figure, in light of the fact that the UAE government has adopted a policy of Emiratization. Not included in it are the illegal immigrants: in 2003 the UAE government issued an amnesty and over 200,000 illegal workers came forward. Whether impoverished or not, all of these people were subject to some form of wage slavery, though they may not be aware of it.

The obvious form of wage slavery includes those holding menial jobs such as factory workers, construction workers, and housecleaners. These are people who come to the UAE and work for what in their home countries would be considered a lot of money. However, their wages, if compared to other wages earned within the UAE, are pitifully low. Some earn only the equivalent of $200 per month which is insufficient to meet the cost of living in the UAE, while sending a portion back to their families.

The factory and construction workers typically live in labor camps which are hurriedly constructed and poor in quality. Several of them are crowded into one room, with a small air-conditioning unit in the ceiling. They are transported daily to and from work in buses that are not air-conditioned, even in summer. Often they are not paid on time, which has led to a few cases of rioting and setting fire to the camps.

It is not unusual to see women dressed in *abayas* with *shaylas* walking a few steps behind an Arab family, pushing a baby carriage or holding an Arab child in their arms. These women, usually Philipino, Indonesian, or Malaysian, work as housekeepers in Arab or expatriate families, and hold next to no rights at all. Locked in the homes where they work, they rarely receive any wages. These women, some of whom are as young as six-year-old girls, are often beaten by their mistresses and sexually abused by their masters. . . .

Because globalization has contributed to the continuation of slavery, albeit in new forms, slavery will not be eradicated without globalization.

It can be argued that these cases are not classic examples of slavery. However, the processes of globalization and modernization require us to re-define slavery: The very nuances and modality of enslaving people have undergone change. Slaves today are no longer captured in war or sold. Although the former can still be found, slavery now refers to the situation of people who out of economic necessity enter into work relationships that either limit their freedom of choice or their mobility. Except for the child who becomes a camel jockey, slavery today is voluntary: willingly but perhaps unknowingly people give up their freedoms.

Those who choose to put themselves in the position of being human traffic for prostitution do so for the most part with the knowledge of what they are doing. They may not realize the conditions they are entering but the prospect of a better life lures them. Unfortunately, this fantasy soon disappears. Similarly, the majority of those who enter into a slave wage contract have no idea of the consequences. The vast majority, whether underprivileged or enjoying apparent privileges, willingly accept the situation in which their freedom is controlled or limited. It is this psychological aspect of the wage slave that turns them into slaves. It is inconceivable that intelligent humans fall prey to the subtle machinations of employers who infuse fears into their minds of losing their livelihood or the chance to return home. These tactics of fear contribute to the ongoing practice of wage slavery.

The question is whether modern day slavery should be condoned or stopped. It is clearly possible to monitor and eradicate the practice of buying children as camel jockeys. In fact, many of the wealthy sheikhs who own the race camels have stopped using children in public. This does not mean that the practice has completely stopped; it may have diminished, but in many instances it has simply been swept under the rug.

But the other two forms of slavery in the UAE will prove more difficult to abolish. The young women who enter into prostitution are not aware of the price they are going to pay or the freedoms they are going to give up. Can this form of slavery be curtailed? Probably it can, but only with improved education and economic conditions for those who involve themselves in such employment. The growing interest of the media and international human rights organizations has brought slavery into the limelight. As more people become aware of what slavery looks like, the practice may perhaps dwindle and fade away as a means to making fast money.

It is the practice of wage slavery that will be most difficult to eradicate, if at all. This voluntary form of slavery is partly created by the global economic conditions. Although the total ramifications of the situation are not always obvious, this condition will prevail so long as people believe they are better off entering into this arrangement for a determined period of time. They endure the fears instilled into them and the mental and at times physical anguish they are subjected to because these are perceived as a means to an end. But among the many who endure there are those who cannot pull themselves out of their situation as they become so indoctrinated with fear of the loss of freedom and mobility. They do not see any other way; they do not perceive themselves as slaves.

In conclusion, slavery in the UAE and other Gulf States can be stopped, but this demands the recognition that slavery persists and the moral courage to change the laws of the land. Ironically, because globalization has contributed to the continuation of slavery, albeit in new forms, slavery will not be eradicated without globalization, for it is only the economically wealthy countries that can do most to combat it: without international pressure it is doubtful that these practices will ever be abolished.

The World Trade Organization's Migrant Worker Policies Worsen Human Trafficking

Basav Sen

Basav Sen is a writer and activist based in Washington, D.C., who works on global economic justice, immigrants' rights, and housing justice issues.

The General Agreement on Trade in Services (GATS), now being negotiated in the World Trade Organization (WTO), is likely to reduce migrant workers to the status of commodities. "Mode 4" of GATS deals with "movement of natural persons," i.e., the migration of people to foreign countries as workers. GATS Mode 4 does not deal with immigration, as in people from one country moving to, and settling down in, another. It deals only with temporary migrants, who go to a foreign country to work for a limited (often specified) time, for a particular job with a particular employer or to fulfill a specific contract. This category of workers is often called guestworkers.

GATS Mode 4—and the system of short-term foreign guestworkers that it promotes—is a threat to both guestworkers themselves and to native-born workers in the countries they work in; it is a threat to longstanding human rights principles; and finally, it is a threat to the long-term development prospects of guestworkers' countries of origin.

Guestworkers: A Growing Global Presence

As of 2003, there were 175 million people worldwide (or about 3% of the world's population) living and working outside of their countries of origin, according to International Labor Organization (ILO) estimates. Of this number, 120 million were guestworkers and their families; the rest were permanent immigrants, refugees, or asylum seekers. The global guestworker population has doubled in less than 30 years and, according to the ILO, will likely double again over the next quarter century.

According to UNESCO [United Nations Educational, Scientific, and Cultural Organization] data, North America, Europe, and Asia are the major destinations of guestworkers, with 23%, 32%, and 28% of the global guestworker population respectively. The United States, Russia, and Germany have the most guestworkers of any country. Some countries, notably in the Persian Gulf region, have a strikingly large population share of guestworkers. In two countries, United Arab Emirates and Kuwait, guestworkers form the majority of the population (74% and 58% respectively). Among countries of origin, Mexico and the Philippines send the most guestworkers abroad.

Guestworkers labor in a wide range of occupations, from highly skilled work (such as doctors and computer engineers) to the so-called 3D jobs (dirty, demeaning, and dangerous) in construction and domestic work. It is hard to construct a global picture of their occupational distribution. Some major recipient countries, such as Germany and Saudi Arabia, provide no data, while others like France provide only incomplete data. For some countries, however, complete data are available. In the United States, 4.8 million migrant workers in 1999 (the latest year for which numbers [were] available [in 2006]) worked as "production workers, transport, equipment operators and labourers" (for example, construction workers), 3 million as service workers (janitors, nannies, security guards), and 2.6 million as professional and technical workers. These figures make clear the wide range of guestworker occupations.

India, Mexico, and the Philippines are the top three recipient countries for remittances, or money that guestworkers send to family members in their home countries—$10 billion, $9.9 billion, and $6.4 billion respectively, according to a 2003 World Bank report. Some countries have a very large share of their Gross Domestic Product (GDP) attributable to remittances—23% for Jordan, 14% for Lebanon and El Salvador.

[The General Agreement on Trade in Services (GATS)] worsens the exploitation of guestworkers as a whole.

At least 15% of the global migrant workforce is undocumented. Undocumented workers are an invisible population, existing outside of host countries' legal framework and therefore highly vulnerable to exploitation by predatory employers. But holding travel documents is no guarantee of legal rights. Often, even documented guestworkers are not entitled to the same legal protections as citizens. In the United States, for example, legal changes enacted in 1996 have removed basic due process protections for both migrant workers and permanent residents. Even when they enjoy the same rights on paper as the citizens of the host country, they may face extra-legal discrimination based on race and national origin.

Across the globe, guestworkers face abuses including not being allowed to join a union or organize for their rights; not getting paid on time, and sometimes not getting paid at all, for work they have performed; unsafe and unhealthy working conditions; wages that are far below the average paid to native-born workers for equivalent work; long hours; and even some recorded cases of confinement and forced labor. The Coalition of Immokalee Workers, an immigrant farm workers' organization based in Florida, has documented several instances of migrant farmworkers being kept under armed watch by their employers, and threatened with death if they tried to leave. . . .

Trading in People

Since guestworkers already face such abusive conditions, it is fair to ask how GATS could possibly make it worse for them. GATS is unlikely to change the circumstances of individual guestworkers. However, it worsens the exploitation of guestworkers as a whole in two fundamental ways. First, the draft GATS agreement erodes even the limited legal protections that are available to guestworkers (whether documented or undocumented) today and blocks the evolution of progressive national and international legal instruments to protect migrant workers' rights. Second, by making it easier for employers to hire guestworkers, GATS could greatly increase the number of exploited migrant workers worldwide.

Guestworkers generally enjoy neither the customary legal rights they are entitled to in their home countries nor those that native-born workers in the host country have. In theory, migrants are covered by legal protections for workers in the countries where they hold citizenship. In practice, that's meaningless: abroad, they lack physical access to the labor unions, legal service and human rights organizations, and courts in their home countries. Even in the extremely unlikely event that a migrant worker succeeds in filing legal proceedings in his or her home country's courts against an employer, those courts would most likely lack jurisdiction because the abuse will have occurred abroad.

It's also quite likely that the employer will be based in a third country, distinct from both the worker's home country and the host country, making the reach of the home-country legal system even more tenuous. For example, an Australian contractor could win a contract in Germany, recruit workers in the Philippines, bring them into Germany under GATS Mode 4, and abuse them with no accountability under Philippines law.

Unfortunately, guestworkers are not likely to be protected by the laws of the host country either. Under the draft GATS Mode 4 agreement, guestworkers will be contractually bound to an employer; they are unlikely to have the right to join a union; and they may even be required by contract to pay their employer for their passage to the host country. Such an exploitative scenario is possible because guestworkers will be classified as "service providers" rather than as workers, and their movement across borders will be regarded as "trade" rather than migration according to draft GATS Mode 4 language, thus excluding them from even the limited protections they may enjoy as migrant workers under ILO provisions or under domestic law in the host country.

Migrants' rights advocates worldwide believe GATS Mode 4 amounts to the creation of a 21st-century system of indentured servitude.

The treatment of guestworkers will probably vary by host country and by circumstance, with some host countries providing marginally more protection. However, in the absence of binding legal commitments to provide protections to guestworkers, host countries are under no obligation to do so and often won't, whether to appease xenophobia at home or out of deference to foreign investors. Even those host countries that wish to protect the rights of guestworkers may not be allowed to do so under GATS. For example, Bjorn Jensen of the American Friends Service Committee observes that requiring wage parity between domestic workers and guestworkers may be seen as protectionist—a violation of WTO rules.

Indentured Servitude

Migrants' rights advocates worldwide believe GATS Mode 4 amounts to the creation of a 21st-century system of indentured servitude. "Rather than reduce migrants to a factor of production, or a commodity to be exported and imported, migration policy must acknowledge migrants as human beings and address their dignity and human rights," according to a joint statement issued by numerous U.S. human rights and immigrant organizations.

Sadly, GATS Mode 4 represents a step backward for migrants' rights. Over the last several decades, the definition and coverage of human rights have expanded significantly, at least on paper, with successive United Nations conferences and conventions on the rights of women, indigenous peoples, and other marginalized populations. For migrant workers, the relevant international instrument is the Convention on Migrant Workers (UNCMW), which has unfortunately been ratified by only 34 countries to date. While this convention does not create any new rights, it explicitly requires governments to apply existing human rights standards, such as those found in the Universal Declaration of Human Rights, to foreign-born migrant workers, whether temporary or permanent and without regard to whether or not they have valid travel documents.

Major host countries such as the United States, Germany, Canada, Saudi Arabia, and Kuwait have not signed the convention, so for now the treaty is largely symbolic. But GATS will render it obsolete before it can be ratified by more countries, preventing it from ever evolving into an effective international legal instrument and undermining decades of work by human rights activists, organized labor, and others to remake global immigration policies in a more humane manner. (According to the 1969 Vienna Convention on the Law of Treaties, a newer treaty or agreement always supersedes an older agreement when the two are in conflict. Therefore, GATS will supersede the UNCMW.) Effectively, GATS is "setting up a separate sphere of migration not based on rights, which works to legitimize the idea that migrant workers don't deserve rights," says Jensen.

Speculation has been rife about what categories of workers GATS Mode 4 will ultimately cover. At present, it appears to be more geared towards the movement of highly skilled workers such as doctors and computer programmers. While the potential for exploitation of these workers is probably less than for unskilled workers, it nevertheless is a concern. The experience of foreign high-tech workers in the United States under the H-1B visa program shows how even skilled workers face lack of job portability (i.e. being contractually tied to one employer) and are vulnerable to layoffs. During the dot-com bust, when firms in the computer industry laid off large numbers of employees, the first to lose their jobs were the foreign workers with H-1B visas.

There is every chance, however, that Mode 4 will be expanded to cover low-skill workers as well. For one thing, governments from countries that rely on guestworkers for most low-skill jobs (such as United Arab Emirates, Kuwait, and Saudi Arabia) as well as from countries that rely heavily on remittances from low-skill emigrants (such as Mexico, El Salvador, and the Philippines) are likely to push hard for expanding Mode 4 to cover a wider range of occupations down the skill ladder. . . .

A Wider Race to the Bottom

Migrant workers are not the only workers threatened by GATS Mode 4. It would give employers the flexibility to cut labor costs by firing their own workers and contracting with a labor supplier who will bring in foreign workers under GATS at lower pay and with very few legal rights. The incentive to save on labor costs and to ensure a docile, easily exploitable workforce is strong, and joblessness is likely to increase in host countries as a consequence. Even the threat of bringing in foreign guestworkers can be used by employers to force unions to accept undesirable contract terms or to compel employees to abandon their efforts to unionize. Manufacturing workers in wealthy countries have been watching their jobs migrate to foreign sweatshops for years, but service workers have been relatively immune from the threat of outsourcing since geographical presence is a prerequisite for many types of services. Under GATS, however, employers will be able to bring the sweatshop home legally, threatening service-sector workers with the same mass layoffs that manufacturing workers have had to deal with.

The migration of highly skilled workers poses its own problems for their countries of origin. Analysts expect that the movement of workers under GATS Mode 4 will typically be from poorer countries to wealthier countries. Workers themselves are more likely to join employers who will relocate them to a wealthier country, in the hope of earning more money to send home. The employing firms stand to make greater profits in wealthier countries as well.

The first and foremost reason that immigrants' rights groups oppose GATS Mode 4 is "because it jeopardizes the well-being and human rights" of immigrants.

GATS thus sets up a "brain drain" scenario, in which poor countries that already lack educated professionals will lose an inordinate number of them to emigration. For a country with a shortage of doctors, of medical colleges to train doctors, and even of people with the educational background to be admitted to medical college, the loss of doctors is disastrous. This in turn has a serious adverse impact on the ability of a poor country to develop its health care infrastructure and provide medical care to its own population. Similarly, the loss of engineers, computer programmers, architects, accountants, and so on will devastate poor countries. . . .

Building a Movement: Do's and Don'ts

In the United States and other wealthy countries, opposition to the draft GATS Mode 4 agreement comes from opposite ends of the political spectrum. Not surprisingly, immigrants' rights and workers' rights organizations are mobilizing against the threats to immigrants' labor rights—and, more fundamentally, their very humanity—embodied in the agreement. But right-wing anti-immigrant organizations have their own criticisms of GATS Mode 4; they oppose any program likely to bring large numbers of foreigners into their country, although they often couch their opposition in other terms. For example, the Center for Immigration Studies, a U.S.-based anti-immigration think tank, takes the position that negotiating guestworker programs in the WTO places the entire framework of U.S. immigration law at risk of being challenged as a "trade barrier" and overturned in the WTO dispute resolution process.

So immigrants' rights groups thus find themselves advocating for a similar outcome as the very same right-wing groups whose broader agenda they are normally battling in the public policy arena. This is an unexpected turn of affairs, one that carries certain risks and responsibilities.

Most immigrants' rights organizations (certainly, all the groups I'm aware of) know better than to attempt to form an alliance of convenience with the right. Beyond merely maintaining their independence from anti-immigrant groups, though, progressive organizations need to articulate a position that is plainly different from the anti-immigrant agenda, and to emphasize this difference at every opportunity. As NNIRR's [National Network for Immigrant and Refugee Rights'] Rajah puts it, the first and foremost reason that immigrants' rights groups oppose GATS Mode 4 is "because it jeopardizes the well-being and human rights" of immigrants; this needs to be articulated again and again so as not to allow progressive opposition to Mode 4 to even unintentionally strengthen the anti-immigrant agenda.

How can progressives win labor support on these issues without pandering to xenophobia? The labor movement in the United States (and other wealthy countries) is legitimately concerned about loss of job security and erosion of working conditions for its membership under the GATS guestworker provisions. The challenge is how to channel these concerns into a progressive movement for the rights of all workers, whether native born or immigrant. According to Rajah, the struggle is not against foreign workers who will swarm our shores and take away our jobs, but rather, against "policies that unjustly drive down worker protections here and abroad, and the incessant demand by corporations for cheap, disposable labor." Jensen echoes this analysis by stressing that all workers need to "question a system that pits workers against each other to work for less and less under worse and worse conditions while allowing top management to earn salaries hundreds of times the average workers' pay." These ideas form the nucleus of a progressive agenda linking immigration and economic justice—an agenda in which the fight against GATS 4 is a small but important part.

[*Editor's note:* GATS Mode 4 was passed.]

Free Trade Agreements Do Not Reduce Human Trafficking

Sarah Lazare

Sarah Lazare is a writer and the project director of Courage to Resist, an organization that supports war resisters.

The U.S.-Jordan Free Trade Agreement has led to widespread human trafficking and forced servitude of guest workers in Jordan, and several prominent U.S. companies are implicated, according to a May [2006] report released by the New York City–based National Labor Committee (NLC).

"I was completely shocked by what I saw in Jordan," says Charles Kernaghan, director of the NLC. "Guest workers had miserable conditions—the worst I've seen."

The report is the product of a year of research by the NLC, a workers' advocacy group, and workers' rights groups and unions based in Bangladesh and the United States. Facing the challenges of government secrecy, restricted access to industrial zones and factory boss intimidation, researchers relied heavily on interviews with workers, conducted in homes and other locations out of earshot of factory bosses, to reconstruct the experiences of guest workers in Jordan.

Their findings are chilling.

False Promises Lure Wage Slaves

The typical narrative begins in the guest worker's country of origin. Jordanian factories run ads in Bangladeshi newspapers announcing jobs that pay high wages, provide healthcare and dormitory board, serve food that is "like the West" and offer a chance to see the country. For a fee of $1,000 to $3,000, Bang-

Sarah Lazare, "Human Trafficking in Jordan," *Multinational Monitor*, May/June 2006.

ladeshis can sign a three-year contract guaranteeing them work when they get to Jordan. Guest workers usually borrow this money, often from the black market because they cannot afford bank accounts, with the understanding that their new jobs will give them the means to pay off their debt.

These job offers prove alluring to Bangladeshis beset by poverty. Wages in the Bangladeshi textile industry average 28 cents an hour, according to a 2005 report by the Harvard Center for Textile and Apparel Research. By comparison, Jordan's minimum wage of 58 cents an hour seems appealing.

When Bangladeshis arrive in Jordan, they are immediately stripped of their passports and identification. This restricts their movement, for if they venture outside of their industrial cities, their undocumented status puts them at risk of being picked up by police, imprisoned and even deported.

The Bangladeshis quickly learn that Jordan's labor standards do not apply to them. Guest workers typically do not receive the legal minimum wage and are often cheated of over half of the wages owed to them. Factory owners commonly require guest workers to labor over 100 hours a week without overtime premium, enforce seven-day workweeks and provide only one to two days off per month. Guest workers tell of being forced to work up to 72-hour shifts and being beaten for falling asleep. If they complain, guest workers are beaten or threatened with deportation. Several guest workers report that they feel like slaves.

Miserable Living Conditions

The decent living conditions promised in the ad also ring hollow. The workers report that dormitories are cramped and dirty, food is insufficient and tasteless, and bathrooms are sanitation nightmares.

A worker at the Al Shahaed Apparel & Textile factory that sews clothes for Wal-mart and K-Mart told the NLC, "We were subjected to punishment when we wanted more food.

The guards used to beat us up with broomsticks. Sometimes they used to force us to stand naked in an air-conditioned room in severe cold."

Workers at Al Safa Factory, which sews clothes for Gloria Vanderbilt, Mossimo and Kohl's, tell of a fellow worker who hung herself after being raped by a plant manager.

When their contracts expire, most guest workers are denied the return ticket promised them by employers and must borrow more money to return to their homes. After three years of dismal pay, combined with exorbitant black market interest rates on loans to secure their positions, workers return to their families saddled with debt.

A majority of Jordan's apparel workers fall through the cracks of whatever worker protections may exist in Jordan.

According to the report, this is the consistent experience for Jordan's estimated 36,500 guest workers, mostly from Bangladesh and China. Kernaghan says that labor violations against guest workers are pervasive in Jordan's estimated 114 garment factories and especially in the roughly half of these that are subcontracting factories. "Working conditions are completely out of control," he says. According to Kernaghan, virtually all Jordanian factories currently do business with U.S. companies, including Wal-Mart, Kohl's, Gloria Vanderbilt, Target, L.L. Bean, Thalia Sodi, K-mart and Victoria's Secret.

The 2001 Trade Agreement

The impetus for the rise of guest worker factories comes from the 2001 U.S.-Jordan Free Trade Agreement, which gives Jordan an advantaged trading position with the United States and has led to a vast expansion of the country's apparel industry.

Ironically, the trade agreement is unique in its inclusion of workers' rights statutes in the main body of its text. Tim Waters, director of rapid response for the United Steelworkers Union, says his union initially endorsed the agreement, heralding it as "a model in protecting workers' rights."

However, according to the report, these protections—which many worker advocates believe are chimerical [illusory] in any case—do not extend to the guest worker class that comprises 67 percent of Jordan's garment industry workforce.

Guest workers have no allies in Jordan. The report states that Jordanian trade unions refuse to help organize foreign workers, and the Bangladeshi embassy in Jordan turned a deaf ear to guest workers' pleas for help. Language barriers also pose significant obstacles.

The report also charges that monitors hired by the brand-name apparel companies and retailers that use the subcontractors fail to uncover dismal working conditions. They give factory owners warning of their arrival and conduct most of their interviews on the factory floor, where workers are told to lie to them about their conditions or face penalties such as beatings or deportation.

Thus, a majority of Jordan's apparel workers fall through the cracks of whatever worker protections may exist in Jordan.

U.S. Companies Also Are to Blame

While the Jordanian government is clearly at fault for its complicity, responsibility for the guest workers' situation, says Kernaghan, rests with, "the U.S. government for overseeing the trade agreement and on the companies for their useless monitoring of factories."

After repeated requests for an interview, Kohl's released a short statement suggesting that the report's charges are unsubstantiated: "To the best of our knowledge, none of these factories [cited in the report] are or have ever produced Kohl's private or exclusive brand merchandise."

Yet, according to Kernaghan, Kohl's was identified by labels that were smuggled out of the guest worker factories by guest workers themselves.

Wal-Mart acknowledges using factories cited in the report, but says it properly inspects them. "Our policy is that when anything is brought to our attention, we will go in and audit and work with that supplier and factory on any issues that were raised," says Beth Keck, director of international corporate affairs for Wal-Mart. When asked how these same auditors could have initially overlooked the severe and widespread labor violations cited in this report, she states, "There are things that you see on a visit, and other times you may not see those things."

Kernaghan says that since the release of the report, several companies have admitted to violations and are engaging in negotiations with the NLC.

Tim Waters attributes corporate abuses to ineffective enforcement of the trade agreement's workers' rights statutes. "A law is only worth anything if it can be enforced. The [George W.] Bush Administration has taken no effort to enforce this law. When humans are trafficked no one even looks into it," he says.

Kernaghan echoes Waters's criticism and is hopeful that the report will lead to better enforcement of laws protecting workers' rights.

However, he suggests that the problem is much deeper. Kernaghan calls the U.S.-Jordan trade agreement "a test case" for free trade, stating, "here is a free trade agreement that unions actually endorsed. This was supposed to be, overall, the best trade agreement for workers."

That even this "model" trade agreement spiraled into human trafficking and indentured servitude is a warning sign about the inherent pressures of such trade agreements, Kernaghan says.

Global Sanctions Do Not Reduce Human Trafficking

Farida Akhter

Farida Akhter is the executive director of Unnayan Bikalper Ni-tinirdharoni Gobeshona (UBINIG), or the Policy Research for Development Alternatives, in Bangladesh. She is the author of Resisting Norplant: Women's Struggle in Bangladesh Against Coercion and Violence.

Human trafficking, particularly of women and children, always has serious political significance. The latest extra concern is the recent threat of the United States to impose sanction against 10 countries including Bangladesh. The control of the movement of people across borders is perceived by the United States as a security concern and linked to its overall strategy of "war against terrorism". It is also clearly linked to its explicit foreign policy of assessing countries as a "failed" or "dysfunctional" state to deny such countries the sovereign existence to rule themselves.

It goes without saying that trafficking in people, particularly women and children, is of grave concern to women's organisations, human rights groups, the media and other activists. In fact, the issue has been raised by these organisations in our country, which have been active in preventing the situations that lead to trafficking and in taking measures once trafficking has occurred. Trafficking has been considered as a violence against women and children because it is related to the sex industry, slave trade, illegal and cross-border marriages, organ trade and so on. Mostly young girls and boys are the victims. It is a trade on human bodies, and often girls fall into prey of the traffickers because of dowry and other forms of social discrimination against women. There is no doubt that

Farida Akhter, "Bangladesh: Threat of Sanction Can't Stop Human Trafficking," *Human Rights Solidarity*, vol. 14, September 2004. Reproduced by permission.

all those countries suffering from such violence would take appropriate measures to stop such crime. It is one of the issues that has at least received attention from all quarters, including the government. Even at the regional forum trafficking is taken seriously in South Asia, where there are source countries, receiving countries and transit countries. On this particular issue, the South Asian governments came together to enact the Convention on Combating Trafficking in Women and Children in Prostitution in 2002.

Human Trafficking Is a World Trade

Yet it is true that trafficking could not be combated as much as desired. Bangladesh is called a "source" country because men, women and children from poorer and vulnerable families are being trafficked to India, Pakistan, the United Arab Emirates [UAE], Europe and America. The people involved in trafficking include village brokers, travel agents and some criminals. They are the agents of traffickers and part of an international syndicate and mafias, which may originate in many developed countries including those in Europe and America. This is a multi-billion dollar global trade.

The present situation in Bangladesh, however, is becoming more complicated. According to the U.S. State Department's "Trafficking in Persons Report 2004" released in Washington on June 14, 600,000 to 800,000 victims of human trafficking are being transported across international borders each year. Bangladesh is identified as a source country from where about 10,000 to 20,000 women and girls are trafficked annually to India, Pakistan, Bahrain, Kuwait and the UAE for the purposes of sexual exploitation, involuntary domestic servitude and debt bondage.

Accordingly, the U.S. State Department blamed Bangladesh for making "no effort" to curb international sex trafficking and put the country into a list of 10 blacklisted countries with the warning that they might face non-trade sanctions. "Unless governments demonstrably improve their records to combat trafficking by October [2004], they will be subjected to sanctions like cut-offs in non-humanitarian and non-trade-related U.S. aid," the United States threatened. Other countries on the same blacklist are Ecuador, North Korea, Venezuela, Burma, Equatorial Guinea, Sierra Leone, Cuba, Guyana and Sudan. Bangladesh is the only new entrant to the list.

The basis of blacklisting countries for making "no effort" is, of course, unilateral on the part of the United States. There have been no prior consultations with the relevant groups except taking information from the USAID [United States Agency for International Development] "funded" non-governmental organisations. The report contains data on human trafficking of 140 countries. The U.S. State Department made a classification of the states in terms of government efforts against the crime. The classification is in tiers: Tier 1 includes 25 countries, which have the best legal and administrative practices against trafficking; in Tier 2 there are 54 countries, which have medium practices against trafficking. But Tier 2 also has a separate watch list for weak practices. About 42 countries are under the list. In Tier 3, there are 10 countries where governments are accused of playing no role in fighting trafficking. Tier 3 countries are also called black-listed countries, which face the threat of U.S. sanctions. Until this year [2004], Bangladesh used to be treated as a Tier 2 nation. But in the latest report, it is under Tier 3. "Corruption of law enforcement agencies and weak governance has pushed the impoverished country further down," the report reads.

While 10 countries are blacklisted with warnings of sanctions, eight countries (Brazil, Cambodia, India, Indonesia, Mexico, Moldova, Sierra Leone and Tanzania) are given US million[s] to "help them fight human trafficking". U.S. President George [W.] Bush reportedly made the announcement on July 16. The news reports said that to underscore U.S. commitment to freeing people from modern-day slavery, Bush selected these countries for the "strategic anti-trafficking in persons assistance" programme.

A Long Criminal Chain

It is also very important to note that while "source" countries are blamed, there is no suggested action against the "receiving" and "user" countries, such as the United States itself. Only the supply side is coerced by the U.S. government actions. If the sex industry and slave trade continue their billion-dollar business, then how will the entire chain stop? Is it only in the hands of the governments to control such trade?

There is a new dimension added in the U.S. report about trafficking, which relates to the use of children in war. This must have resulted from the U.S. government's fear of certain countries that are against the U.S. war[s] in Iraq and Afghanistan. It may be noticed in the U.S. report that tens of thousands of trafficked children are forced to serve in government armies, armed militias and rebel groups. The problem is most critical in Africa and Asia. Armed groups in the Americas, Eurasia and the Middle East also use children.

It is not at all proved anywhere in the world that sanctions can improve the situation.

"Some children have been used for suicide missions or are forced to commit atrocities against their families and communities. Others, including some of the 15,000 involved in recent Liberian conflicts, are made to serve as porters, cooks, guards, servants, messengers or spies. Many child soldiers, mostly girls, are sexually abused," the report states.

However, the report shows trafficking from Bangladesh are for the purposes of sexual exploitation, involuntary domestic servitude and debt bondage. A small number of women and girls are trafficked through Bangladesh from Burma to India. Bangladeshi boys are also trafficked into the UAE and Qatar and forced to work as camel jockeys and beggars. Women and children from rural areas in Bangladesh are trafficked to urban centres for commercial sexual exploitation and domestic work. That means the U.S. report did not identify Bangladeshi children as being used for suicide bombing or by any rebel.

In a press conference on June 30, [2004], U.S. Ambassador in Bangladesh Harry K. Thomas, who communicated the U.S. warning to the Bangladeshi government, reiterated the U.S. concerns over the grave human trafficking situation in Bangladesh that might lead to sanctions on non-humanitarian and non-trade sectors. "It (Bangladesh) failed to make significant efforts to prosecute traffickers and address the complicity of government officials in trafficking," he said. Thomas observed that the report was critical of police cooperation with traffickers and the failure to arrest these policemen, substantial decline in convictions and failure of the "speedy trial" anti-trafficking court to convict a single trafficker. He expressed concern over the misuse of funds provided for victims of human trafficking and internal corruption issues within the police and the judiciary. However, he gave hope with the warnings that Bangladesh would be moved back to Tier 2 if the government made further efforts to implement actions to combat human trafficking.

The criminal chain is long, beginning from Bangladesh to countries in Europe and America. Who will prosecute these countries?

Now it seems that Bangladesh has to prove its commitment to fight the crime of trafficking in people by making more prosecutions within a "certain time period set by the U.S. government". The Bangladeshi government must take actions and give a report on its performance. If the U.S. government is satisfied, then the threat of sanction may be lifted; otherwise there will be definite sanctions.

It is not at all proved anywhere in the world that sanctions can improve the situation. In fact, the Harkin Bill against Child Labour has contributed to further trafficking in children as they lost jobs in the garment factories and became more vulnerable to trafficking.

People's Vulnerabilities

Bangladesh is one of the countries in South Asia that has been facing the problems of trafficking for the last few decades. But that has very clear connections between globalisation and the booming sex industry worldwide. Human trafficking cannot be stopped without understanding how the capitalist patriarchy, phenomenon of modernisation, concept of nation state, militarisation, war, concept of development and growth model are contributing to the increase in this trade. It is an outcome of the social, economic and environmental vulnerabilities of people that are caused by globalisation. Even wars in different countries are causing displacement of people and part of it is leading to trafficking. Globalisation has encouraged free mobility of capital, technology, experts and sex tourists. This has created a demand for trafficking in women and children for commercial gains. The testimonies of the victims of trafficking expressed in the South Asia Court of Women, which was held in Bangladesh on August 12 [2004], showed clearly how the flesh trade happened due to vulnerabilities of poor people.

Trafficking is the worst form of violation of human rights. It must be stopped whatever the numerical figures are. There is global resistance against trafficking and the real causes of trafficking have to be traced so that it can really be stopped. The SAARC [South Asian Association for Regional Cooperation] Peoples' Forum has analysed in its meetings that the issues of livelihood and food insecurity are linked to human trafficking, particularly of women and children. Environmental degradation, ecological erosion and destruction of biodiversity based on production systems further accelerate the process. So one cannot blame the people moving out in search of food and work. The criminal traffickers are taking advantage of the situation and making business on these vulnerabilities. But the approach to combat trafficking cannot be only "finding" and "prosecuting" criminals within Bangladesh. The criminal chain is long, beginning from Bangladesh to countries in Europe and America. Who will prosecute these countries?

Measures have to be taken for prevention rather than only targeting the criminals of trafficking. It must be acknowledged that the media's reporting and social activities on creation of awareness have been effective in making people aware of the deceptive mechanisms adopted by the agents of trafficking. On the other hand, the government must take measures by which people have complete control over food and livelihood. However, we would also like to make a warning. We do not want "restriction" on the free movement of people. People must be ensured of secured movement.

CHAPTER 4

What Role Do Victims Play in Human Trafficking?

Chapter Preface

According to the Virginia-based Tahirih Justice Center, between 9,500 and 14,000 American men used an international marriage service to meet their spouses in 2004. Once referred to as mail-order brides, because they were featured in paper catalogues sent through the mail, women seeking husbands from abroad now find their mates online and through services known as marriage brokers. Although many of the women and men who find spouses through brokers defend their right to use them, many organizations and even governments have adopted policies against what some opponents consider legalized human trafficking.

Millions of women have turned to men in other nations as a means of escaping harsh conditions in their countries of origin. One way for them to find men who are also looking for foreign spouses is through marriage brokers. Unfortunately, in some cases these women are victimized by their new husbands and even by the brokers, some of whom sell the women to foreign men for a steep profit. In a March 2006 article in WeNews.com, Layli Miller-Muro, executive director of the Tahirih Justice Center, notes, "This industry predominantly places women at a disadvantage where the man is the paying client and the woman advertised as a product, a commodity, [which creates a] presumption of power and a potentially very dangerous recipe for abuse." For example, in 2004 Nataliya Fox won a lawsuit against the Maryland-based company Encounters International after she was battered by the husband she met through their service. She won on the grounds that the company did not screen her husband well and did not inform her of her rights as an immigrant, requirements now enforced by the International Marriage Broker Regulation Act of 2005 (IMBRA).

Despite Fox's experience, many people defend the services provided by international marriage brokers, especially the brokers themselves, who believe that theirs should be treated like any other business. In response to the passage of IMBRA in 2005, Natasha Spivack, owner of Encounters International, declared, "American men don't need background checks to marry American women, so the law is discriminatory." Brokers are not alone in their lament regarding the law. Wendy McElroy, a columnist for ifeminist.com, responded to the law by saying, "The IMBRA requires American men who wish to correspond with foreign women through private for-profit matchmaking agencies to first provide those businesses with their police records and other personal information to be turned over to the women." She adds, "Now American men who wish to pursue a legal activity must release their government files to a foreign business and foreign individuals for their personal benefit."

Some of the authors in the following chapter assert that women who turn to marriage brokers as a means of fleeing their desperate conditions may play some role in their own victimization. However, many opponents of marriage brokering argue that the women are duped into believing that they will have a better life abroad. Although no clear data exist to support the number of successful marriages created through these services, it is certain that these companies will continue to operate within and outside of international laws.

Victims of Human Trafficking Are Not to Blame for Their Misery

Carollann Gamino

Carollann Gamino is an intern at Work of Women—WOW!, a subsidiary of World Neighbors, an international development organization striving to eliminate hunger, poverty, and disease.

Although most people around the world believe that slavery ended centuries ago, the reality is that millions of people are forced into and exploited in a modern day slave trade every day. Human trafficking is the world's second largest criminal enterprise, tying with the arms trade and falling closely behind the illegal drug industry, yet it goes strikingly unnoticed by much of the population. Unlike drugs or arms, however, humans can be used, sold, and exploited over and over again for years until the victims finally die of disease, malnutrition, abuse, or murder, or, more rarely, are rescued or escape. The trafficking-in-persons industry has been estimated to generate $5 [billion] to $9 billion per year worldwide.

The International Labour Organization (ILO) estimates that around 12.3 million people across the globe are kept in forced or bonded labor and sexual servitude at any given time. The vast majority of these people are women who are enslaved in the sex industry and exploited because of gender inequality and their vulnerability. According to the U.S. government's *2008 Trafficking in Persons Report*, which is the most comprehensive worldwide report on governmental efforts to combat human trafficking, between 600,000 and 800,000 people are reportedly trafficked across international borders for forced labor and sexual exploitation each year.

That number, however, does not include the millions of people who are enslaved and exploited in their own countries. This is a problem that undoubtedly plagues women at the highest rate. Approximately 80 percent of transnational trafficking victims are women and girls, and up to 50 percent of the victims are children under the age of 18. The Council of Europe has declared that over the past decade human trafficking has reached epidemic proportions.

For Sunita Shaha, a 16-year-old girl from Bhamarpur village in Nepal, these statistics became a reality. Lured in by false affections and words of love, Sunita believed she was falling in love with Laxman Shaha, a man who promised to marry her and whisk her off to Calcutta, India, away from the poverty and rural life in her small village. Laxman convinced Sunita to run away with him without giving word to her parents. Like so many teenage girls, ideas of romance and adventure got the better of her and the two set off for India. However, as is the plight of so many deceived young girls, the "honeymoon" quickly ended and within days of arriving in India, Laxman sold Sunita to a local brothel and left her.

Victims of human trafficking . . . are victims of extreme poverty, oppressive and corrupt governments, and impossible lives.

Stories such as Sunita's are not confined to Nepal, India or any one place. It is not only poor, teenage girls who fall victim. Rather, human trafficking is a problem that does not discriminate against race, nationality, economic or social status, religion, age or gender. It is not confined to one region of the world and it is not committed by one identifiable group of people. Victims are often targeted by networks of small, specialized predators, each with their own area of expertise in coercion, abduction, transportation, sales or exploitation. These predators can be found anywhere from homelessness to high-ranking political positions. Human trafficking is present in all parts of the world, in every country and every region. It is not confined to major cities or rural areas. Offenders and victims have been discovered in operations in U.S. suburbs, Indonesian slums, under Cambodian bridges and in the heart of London. It is a crime that attacks the essence of what it means to be human, and it knows no boundaries.

Poverty Is a Catalyst

One of the primary factors playing into zones of heavy trafficking, however, is poverty. Victims are often from impoverished areas and are promised opportunities for a better life in more developed countries. They are lured with stories of available jobs such as housekeeping, waitressing, or babysitting in wealthier countries, which could presumably lead them to independence, success and a way out of poverty and despair. Many girls like Sunita, are looking for a loving husband, marriage and a life to be proud of. Instead, they find themselves deceived, enslaved and abused.

It is vitally important to recognize the victims as victims, because ... even if they are able to escape, many are unable to return home.

Children are often sold by their own families living in conditions of extreme poverty. Undercover traffickers will offer the parents a "substantial" sum (one they will likely never hand over) in exchange for their children's labor. The parents are told that the children will go to work and live in better conditions than they are currently living in. In reality, the children are forced into inhumane, often unbearable, working conditions. When they arrive in their new "promised land," they are commonly forced into commercial sexual exploitation, such as prostitution or the sex entertainment industry, or they are enslaved in domestic servitude, sweatshop factory work or migrant agricultural work with little to no possibility of returning home.

Victims of human trafficking, such as Sunita, are not to blame in these situations. Rather, they are victims of extreme poverty, oppressive and corrupt governments, and impossible lives. Unlike the vast majority of trafficking victims, Sunita's fate was not sealed. She was able to contact her uncle who happened to be living in Calcutta. Luckily for Sunita, he was able to help her escape from the brothel and find a good husband in India. Although she found a better life, Sunita, like so many trafficking victims, did not return home.

Misconceptions Lead to Further Threats

Although Sunita fell victim to the horrors of sexual slavery, she did manage to escape one of the worst sides of trafficking: HIV/AIDS. The prevalence of HIV/AIDS in human trafficking is creating devastating consequences. Human trafficking and forced sexual exploitation is blamed for a great deal of the rise of HIV/AIDS in some countries. HIV/AIDS is transported at a dramatically higher rate in trafficking. When the victims are being raped they have no say in the use of condoms nor do they have access to them and often times their assailants refuse to use protection. Furthermore, because children are often falsely believed to be HIV negative, there has been an increase in child trafficking and sexual exploitation. Adult men will often seek out children with the belief that they will not contract HIV/AIDS because children have been exploited less because of their young age, therefore they believe the children will not be HIV positive. Women, because they have been exploited many more times by more men, are believed to have and often do have a higher likelihood of being HIV positive. In Bangladesh, for example, there is a direct correlation between the ages of those infected with HIV/AIDS and the ages of trafficking victims, suggesting a direct relationship between the two. In large part due to this correlation, the average life expectancy of a victim once she has been trafficked is seven years.

As Sunita's uncle realized, it is vitally important to recognize the victims as victims, because, like Sunita, even if they are able to escape, many are unable to return home. Many victims are hundreds of miles and many borders from home. Often times their travel documents are confiscated as a way for their captors to keep them in bondage. Furthermore, an attempt to travel long distances alone with no money or assistance may land them in the very situation they just escaped from. Governments and law enforcement agencies are often untrained with regards to identifying trafficking victims or are simply too corrupt to help the victims return to normal life.

Another barrier may be the very community the victim once called home. Too many victims are never allowed to return to normal life because of social stigmas and misplaced disgust. Due to gender inequality and lack of education, many communities blame the victim for rape and sexual exploitation, thereby ostracizing the victims themselves, rather than the perpetrators of the exploitation. Furthermore, women victims are often deemed "tainted" by potential husbands and have difficulty finding a stable life. However, the more educated people are about the horrors of trafficking, the more they will be able to embrace, help and protect the victims.

Sex Trafficking in Southeast Asia

While two-thirds (between 200,000 and 400,000) of all women being trafficked for sexual exploitation are from Eastern Europe, the majority of child trafficking cases are in Asia. There are an estimated 300,000 young women and children involved in the sex trade in Southeast Asia. In South Asia, India alone hosts the selling of approximately 200,000 Nepalese girls, many under 14, into the sex slave trade. Nepalese girls are considered the most desirable (and controllable) in India and surrounding areas because of their fair skin and gentle, reserved demeanors, making Nepal one of the most heavily trafficked countries. In addition to this, due to years of conflict, political unrest, and a decreasing availability of jobs or economic opportunity, trafficking from Nepal to India for sexual exploitation has been deemed the busiest "slave traffic" of its nature anywhere in the world.

When Albina Herman was 15 years old, she learned this first hand. As a young orphan from a very poor family, Albina began to work as a domestic helper for a wealthier family in her village. However, it was not long before Albina began to fall victim to sexual exploitation by a member of the house. After this went on for some time, Albina was finally told to leave the home. Although this meant the end of her sexual abuse in that house, Albina was now homeless with no money, no resources and no one to help her. Like so many impoverished children, Albina was easily lured with the false prospect of a new job in India, which she accepted and began the trek with her captor to the Nepal-India border.

Nepal has a 1,740 mile-long open border with India that remains very permeable, enhanced by a free entry and exit system for the citizens of both countries. This has essentially made the trafficking of girls and women hurdle-free. Furthermore, low education levels and a high rate of illiteracy, poverty and low employment opportunities in rural areas play a large role in the increasing trafficking business. As in many parts of the world, impoverished girls and women, often from ethnic minority groups, with little economic opportunities are the most heavily targeted by traffickers. These girls and women often come from families, disrupted by the recent violence, political upheaval and diminishing economic opportunities, and lack the understanding and capacity to exercise their legal rights. The low social status of women and girls, difficulty of enforcing laws against trafficking, polygamy (though officially illegal in Nepal), domestic violence and political corruption all play a role in allowing the trafficking problem to go largely overlooked and unrestrained. The most common trafficking areas in Nepal are isolated rural districts in the central region of the country.

There are several different ways that women and girls fall victim to trafficking in Nepal. First of all, although trafficking and migration are not the same, oftentimes people such as Albina migrating for work purposes fall victim to human trafficking. Nepalese women workers migrating to India do not need to undergo any legal processing, nor do they have to get pre-departure training for prescribed work and/or a proper orientation. Therefore, they are often exploited in the receiving country. The problem is furthered by the procurer-pimp-police networks that make the trafficking process even smoother.

Since involvement in the sex trade . . . is looked upon as a very heinous and shameful act, Nepalese people often have difficulty understanding or accepting the victims' situations.

However, there are still police and border patrol agents who remain uncorrupted and are dedicated to thwarting the human trafficking industry. Luckily for Albina, her captor chose the wrong place to cross the border from Nepal into India. So many traffickers are able to pay off police or are simply not questioned at all when travelling with young, undocumented girls. The police Albina encountered were not so passive. When they saw Albina and her captor, they suspected trafficking and began to interrogate him. Quickly the man tried to escape, but the police were able to rescue Albina and keep her in their custody.

Communities Enable Exploitation

Other sources of trafficking stem from old traditions in which women and girls have little to no value or rights. In communities in certain geographic locations, parents will sometimes sell their daughters and husbands will sell their young unwanted wives to brothels in order to get rid of them. Furthermore, in Nepal there is an old system, called "deuki," (India has a similar system called "devadasi") where families will offer a young girl to a temple to gain religious benefits. After the girl is dedicated, she is most often sold to the highest bidder or used as a temple prostitute. When rich families are childless, they will buy girls from poor rural families and offer them to the temples. These girls will not marry and are forced into prostitution. Although this practice is illegal and is in decline, thousands of girls are still dedicated annually.

Since involvement in the sex trade (even as a victim of enslaved prostitution) is looked upon as a very heinous and shameful act, Nepalese people often have difficulty understanding or accepting the victims' situations. In the rare case that a girl or woman is rescued or returns from being trafficked in the slave trade, there is such shame associated with any form of sexual indiscretion, forced or not, that she often does not want to face her family, relatives or community. Nor do the victims' own families often accept them back because of the social insult or stigma that is associated with the atrocity. Rather, families tend to wish that their trafficked daughters had never come back rather than joyfully accept them and help to rehabilitate them; and in the case of a trafficked wife, her husband will never accept her back. Considering this, one can imagine the impact of trafficking on society.

Albina, having no parents and no safe family to return to, unlike many victims who are simply ostracized and rejected by their families, was referred by the police to a nongovernmental organization (NGO) that works to combat the trafficking of women and girls. Albina was taken under the wings of the NGO and went to its rehabilitation center in Kathmandu, where she received counseling, learned to stitch clothing, and was given food, clothing and medical treatment. After three years of rehabilitation and training, the NGO will help Albina find a job and get her settled into a safe and stable life.

Many Trafficking Victims Do Not Cooperate with Officials

José Cardenas

José Cardenas is a staff writer for the St. Petersburg Times.

Two years ago [in 2005], immigration officers asked Ida Lopez to help a woman rescued from a forced-prostitution operation in Tampa [Florida].

Lopez, a worker with the New Port Richey arm of the nonprofit group World Relief, found social services for the 25-year-old woman from Mexico.

Human traffickers had brought her to Tampa with the promise of a job in a factory.

"She said she couldn't sleep at night waiting for them to say, 'There's a client waiting,'" said Lopez, 29, a political refugee from Cuba. "I cried with her."

But local investigators are finding that victims of human trafficking don't surface easily.

In the six months since World Relief got a $450,000 grant from the U.S. Department of Justice to help survivors in the region, none have been found.

Still, the grant is part of a new awareness of human trafficking taking shape in Tampa Bay.

Last fall [2006], the Clearwater Police Department also received a $450,000 grant from the Justice Department.

Clearwater Detective James McBride is the only law enforcement officer in Tampa Bay dedicated entirely to investigating human trafficking, said Deputy Police Chief Dewey Williams.

Trafficking Is Not Smuggling

Trafficking in people is not the same as smuggling them.

Smugglers typically are paid to take people illegally across international borders, leaving them alone once they arrive.

But while traffickers may take people across borders, they exploit their victims, making money by forcing them into slavery, involuntary servitude or the commercial sex industry.

After drug dealing, human trafficking is tied with illegal arms sales as the second-largest criminal industry in the world, according to the Health and Human Services Department.

Following the lead of Collier and Lee counties, Clearwater police has formed the Clearwater Area Task Force on Human Trafficking.

It's made up of law enforcement agencies, prosecutors and social services on both sides of the bay.

The Florida Coalition Against Human Trafficking based in Lee County also received a $2-million grant from the U.S. Department of Health and Human Services late last year [2006].

Victims are unlikely to come forward on their own because often they are undocumented immigrants who fear both the traffickers and law enforcement.

That grant will establish a "Rescue and Restore" campaign in Tampa and other Florida cities.

The goal is to show health-care providers, social service organizations and law enforcement agencies how to identify victims of human trafficking.

Much of that grant is also to be disbursed among grass roots social service agencies to provide care for survivors.

"In Tampa we have gotten the most response out of anywhere in Florida as far as volunteers," said Ashley Wilson of the Florida Coalition.

A Community of Awareness

In Clearwater, creating community awareness will be key, Dewey said.

Victims are unlikely to come forward on their own because often they are undocumented immigrants who fear both the traffickers and law enforcement.

"As we go through the community we run into people who just don't understand what this is and can't fathom that it happens here," said Williams.

Clearwater officers first suspected human trafficking after they raided a brothel in 2001, but they did not prove that human trafficking had taken place.

Still, the case may have convinced federal officials that Clearwater is a good place to investigate, said Terry Coonan, executive director of the Center for the Advancement of Human Rights at Florida State University.

"Clearwater and all these cities are getting the grants so they can find out where are all the cases," Coonan said.

The extent of human trafficking nationally is unknown.

But the issue is pressing enough that Florida is one of two dozen states that have added anti–human trafficking laws recently. All new police officers in this state must take a course on the topic.

The Justice Department says it has prosecuted 386 traffickers since federal statutes were instituted in 2001.

Investigations and prosecutions are not rare in Florida, where immigrants work in areas such as construction, agriculture and tourism.

Dewey said the Clearwater department has at least four open investigations.

Doug Molloy, chief assistant U.S. Attorney in Fort Myers, said he has 11 open investigations.

"The Clearwater project I think ultimately will be very successful," Molloy said. "The more you make the community aware, the more they are able to recognize what they may not have known as human trafficking before."

Finding Victims Is Difficult

But finding victims in Clearwater and elsewhere remains a formidable challenge.

One of the main goals of the Clearwater task force is to help victims obtain T-Visas.

The visas were first made available in 2000. They give victims of human trafficking legal status if they help law enforcement prosecute perpetrators.

But although 5,000 visas are available each year, only 886 have been approved nationwide since 2002.

To get the visas, victims must show they were subjected to a "severe form" of human trafficking and would face "extreme hardship" if they returned to their country.

Those are tough standards to meet, said Gulf Coast Legal Services attorney Kathlyn Mackovjak, who works with Clearwater police on the human trafficking issue.

Also, Mackovjak said, the Department of Homeland Security is years late in drafting guidelines for how T-Visa holders can receive permanent residency.

Consequently, the lawyer said, immigrants are left uncertain as to whether they will be legalized permanently.

"It's unclear if they are going to extend that status once it runs out," Mackovjak said.

The visa limitations notwithstanding, Dewey said community awareness is already paying off.

"The level of awareness in the Tampa Bay Area is a lot higher than when we started," he said.

Some Trafficking Victims Blame Themselves

Win Naing

Win Naing writes for the Amyinthit news agency, which is based in Chiang Mai, Thailand.

A Burmese woman sits on the wooden floor of a small room in Ranong, a Thai town bordering southern-most Burma. Over the sound of a whirring fan, the 18-year-old, who is just over four feet tall, recounts her past.

"I was sold twice to brothel houses," says Mi Kay (not her real name). She lowers her head and is silent for a while.

Mi Kay ran away from her hometown, Rangoon, more than a year ago. She had eloped with her boyfriend after passing her matriculation exam, but their families forced the couple apart after two days together.

Unhappy and restricted by her family, Mi Kay fled to the southern port town of Kaw Thaung, along the Thai-Burmese border. It was not an unknown place to her, having visited the town as a child.

However, Mi Kay did not know that Kaw Thaung—like many Burmese border towns—was a centre for human trafficking. She worked as a waitress at a local teashop for more than a month before she became a target for human traffickers.

Betrayal and Loss

An older schoolmate from Rangoon came and struck up a conversation one day. The woman lived in Ranong, a Thai border town three kilometres from Kaw Thaung. She told Mi

Kay that there were good jobs across the border. After a few visits from her schoolmate, Mi Kay decided to move.

But Mi Kay's old acquaintance turned out to be a trafficker and sold Mi Kay for 6,000 baht (154 U.S. dollars) to a brothel in Ranong.

Mi Kay at first refused to work, so the brothel owner physically abused and tortured her, breaking her spirit. Finally, she became a sex worker. "It was painful. I was also really afraid as well," she recalls.

Mi Kay works in a well-known red-light area called Pauk Khaung in southern Ranong province, a major fishing industry town in Thailand.

Each evening, the sounds of Burmese karaoke fill the streets in Pauk Khaung. Over 100,000 Burmese migrant workers live in Ranong district. There are about 150 Burmese sex workers at 40 karaoke bars and brothels in Ranong, locals here say. They receive half the 200 to 500 baht (five to 12.80 dollars) paid to the owner for each customer.

Mi Kay described as hell the first four months she spent in isolation at the brothel. "I always thought to run away, but they locked me in during daytime," she says.

Trafficked Burmese women almost never gain their freedom as they are continuously sold between brothels.

Mi Kay once tried to escape, was caught as she waited for a boat back to Burma. "They beat me several times. Both of my hands were swollen," she says, holding up her tiny hands.

Eventually, her brothel owner sold her to another brothel for 10,000 baht (256 dollars). It was a turning point for Mi Kay. The new brothel owner assured her that if she paid off her purchase price, he would let her go. "Sometimes I slept with ten customers in one day to pay the debt," she says. It was repaid in just over a month.

Mi Kay is free to go now, but after all this time of being in the sex industry, she says she cannot. She thinks that being a sex worker is a means of survival and of earning more money for her return home.

The sale of women to brothels is not an unusual story amidst the Burmese community in Ranong, says Thiri, a friend of Mi Kay's. Trafficked Burmese women almost never gain their freedom as they are continuously sold between brothels, she adds.

The Need to Work

Thiri, 33, has been a sex worker for five years. She has HIV, but cannot stop working. "I have to work for income," she explains.

HIV and other sexually transmitted diseases are but some of the vulnerabilities that Burmese sex workers face in Ranong, says health worker Hla Hla Win, who runs a private medical clinic.

She says local authorities from the Burmese side in Kaw Thaung ignore the activities of human trafficking networks, while the Burmese government's actions to eliminate human trafficking are just "window dressing."

Of the newcomers to the sex industry in Ranong [in 2005], almost half of the Burmese entering brothels were trafficked, says Hla Hla Win, also a member of exiled Burmese Women's Union.

Chaw Chaw, anti-trafficking coordinator for the World Vision non-governmental organisation in Rangoon, says the root causes of migration to Thailand are economic, social and political problems in Burma. "Lack . . . of education and general knowledge of travel process (are) part of the main reasons for human trafficking," she says.

Making Trafficking a Priority

Despite international scepticism about the Burmese government's efforts against trafficking, Chaw Chaw says the military regime, called the State Peace and Development Council [SPDC], made this issue part of its national agenda in the last year [2004].

A member of the Myanmar National Committee for Women's Affairs, an SPDC-controlled organisation, recently expressed concern over Burma's human trafficking situation. However the official, who declined to be named, said that trafficking could not just be stopped: "It is a long process. We can only reduce it."

For months, Burmese state television has been running a campaign encouraging people not to go to neighbouring countries and offering suggestions to women on how to avoid traffickers.

Burma's Home Affairs Ministry says the government has "taken action against offenders in 412 cases" of human trafficking between July 2002 and June 2004. It claims to have rescued 1,047 women from being sold abroad in the same period.

Meantime, Mi Kay blames herself for her nightmare. "It was a big mistake to come here," she says, taking a deep breath. "If I did not run away from home, I would not be like this."

Mi Kay says she still loves her boyfriend but has given up on her love because "I have a dirty body."

She still has dreams of returning to Rangoon and to her family. For now, though, she continues working in Ranong. "I do not have enough money yet," she says.

Victims of Human Trafficking Are the Responsibility of the World Community

Pope Benedict XVI

Pope Benedict XVI is the head of the Roman Catholic Church.

The theme of the World Day of Migrants and Refugees invites us this year [2008] to reflect in particular on young migrants. As a matter of fact, the daily news often speaks about them. The vast globalization process underway around the world brings a need for mobility, which also induces many young people to emigrate and live far from their families and their countries. The result is that many times the young people endowed with the best intellectual resources leave their countries of origin, while in the countries that receive the migrants, laws are in force that make their actual insertion difficult. In fact, the phenomenon of emigration is becoming ever more widespread and includes a growing number of people from every social condition. Rightly, therefore, the public institutions, humanitarian organizations and also the Catholic Church are dedicating many of their resources to helping these people in difficulty.

For the young migrants, the problems of the so-called "difficulty of dual belonging" seem to be felt in a particular way: on the one hand, they feel a strong need to not lose their culture of origin, while on the other, the understandable desire emerges in them to be inserted organically into the society that receives them, but without this implying a complete assimilation and the resulting loss of their ancestral traditions. Among the young people, there are also girls who fall victim more easily to exploitation, moral forms of blackmail, and even abuses of all kinds. What can we say, then, about the adolescents, the unaccompanied minors that make up a category at risk among those who ask for asylum? These boys and girls often end up on the street abandoned to themselves and prey to unscrupulous exploiters who often transform them into the object of physical, moral and sexual violence.

Everyone's commitment—teachers, families and students—will surely contribute to helping the young migrants to face in the best way possible the challenge of integration.

Next, looking more closely at the sector of forced migrants, refugees and the victims of human trafficking, we unhappily find many children and adolescents too. On this subject it is impossible to remain silent before the distressing images of the great refugee camps present in different parts of the world. How can we not think that these little beings have come into the world with the same legitimate expectations of happiness as the others? And, at the same time, how can we not remember that childhood and adolescence are fundamentally important stages for the development of a man and a woman that require stability, serenity and security? These children and adolescents have only had as their life experience the permanent, compulsory "camps" where they are segregated, far from inhabited towns, with no possibility normally to attend school. How can they look to the future with confidence? While it is true that much is being done for them, even greater commitment is still needed to help them by creating suitable hospitality and formative structures.

Responding to Their Needs

Precisely from this perspective the question is raised of how to respond to the expectations of the young migrants? What can be done to help them? Of course, it is necessary to aim first of all at support for the family and schools. But how complex the situations are, and how numerous the difficulties these young people encounter in their family and school contexts! In families, the traditional roles that existed in the countries of origin have broken down, and a clash is often seen between parents still tied to their culture and children quickly acculturated in the new social contexts. Likewise, the difficulty should not be underestimated which the young people find in getting inserted into the educational course of study in force in the country where they are hosted. Therefore, the scholastic system itself should take their conditions into consideration and provide specific formative paths of integration for the immigrant boys and girls that are suited to their needs. The commitment will also be important to create a climate of mutual respect and dialogue among all the students in the classrooms based on the universal principles and values that are common to all cultures. Everyone's commitment—teachers, families and students—will surely contribute to helping the young migrants to face in the best way possible the challenge of integration and offer them the possibility to acquire what can aid their human, cultural and professional formation. This holds even more for the young refugees for whom adequate programs will have to be prepared, both in the scholastic and the work contexts, in order to guarantee their preparation and provide the necessary bases for a correct insertion into the new social, cultural and professional world.

The Church looks with very particular attention at the world of migrants and asks those who have received a Christian formation in their countries of origin to make this heritage of faith and evangelical values bear fruit in order to offer a consistent witness in the different life contexts. Precisely in this regard, I invite the ecclesial host communities to welcome the young and very young people with their parents with sympathy, and to try to understand the vicissitudes of their lives and favor their insertion.

Foreign Students Involved Locally

Then, among the migrants, as I wrote in last year's Message, there is one category to consider in a special way: the students from other countries who because of their studies, are far from home. Their number is growing constantly: they are young people who need a specific pastoral care because they are not just students, like all the rest, but also temporary migrants. They often feel alone under the pressure of their studies and sometimes they are also constricted by economic difficulties. The Church, in her maternal concern, looks at them with affection and tries to put specific pastoral and social interventions into action that will take the great resources of their youth into consideration. It is necessary to help them find a way to open up to the dynamism of interculturality and be enriched in their contact with other students of different cultures and religions. For young Christians, this study and formation experience can be a useful area for the maturation of their faith, a stimulus to be open to the universalism that is a constitutive element of the Catholic Church.

Dear young migrants, prepare yourselves to build together [with] your young peers a more just and fraternal society by fulfilling your duties scrupulously and seriously towards your families and the State. Be respectful of the laws and never let yourselves be carried away by hatred and violence. Try instead to be protagonists as of now of a world where understanding and solidarity, justice and peace will reign. To you, in particular, young believers, I ask you to profit from your period of studies to grow in knowledge and love of Christ. Jesus wants you to be his true friends, and for this it is necessary for you to cultivate a close relationship with Him constantly in prayer and docile listening to his Word. He wants you to be his witnesses, and for this it is necessary for you to be committed to living the Gospel courageously and expressing it in concrete acts of love of God and generous service to your brothers and sisters. The Church needs you too and is counting on your contribution. You can play a very providential role in the current context of evangelization. Coming from different cultures, but all united by belonging to the one Church of Christ, you can show that the Gospel is alive and suited to every situation; it is an old and ever new message. It is a word of hope and salvation for the people of all races and cultures, of all ages and eras.

To Mary, the Mother of all humanity, and to Joseph, her most chaste spouse, who were both refugees together with Jesus in Egypt, I entrust each one of you, your families, those who take care of the vast world of young migrants in various ways, the volunteers and pastoral workers that are by your side with their willingness and friendly support.

May the Lord always be close to you and your families so that together you can overcome the obstacles and the material and spiritual difficulties you encounter on your way. I accompany these wishes with a special Apostolic Blessing for each one of you and for those who are dear to you.

Hopes for a Better Future Lure Many Victims into Trafficking Rings

John Celock

John Celock is a New York–based writer who specializes in politics, education, religion, and public policy.

Growing up in rural Zambia, Given Kachepa saw a future containing the possibility of a dollar a day job, if he was lucky to find one, while avoiding the ever-present plagues of HIV and tuberculosis. Orphaned at age 11, Kachepa saw his faith as a way out of the hardships of his life.

Encouraged by his cousins to join the church choir after his parents died, Kachepa viewed choir singing as a refuge from the harsh life he was living. He saw it as a way to get closer to God and to his faith.

"I used to go to church every Sunday, with Bible study and there would be days that I would pray for hours and hours," he said. "I was excited, I will never forget the day that I received Jesus Christ. There were things that I did where I could see God working in my life."

The Look of Modern Slavery

Kachepa thought his faith would lead him to a better life in the United States. When he was 13 he was approached by TTT Partners in Education, a church ministry group from Texas to participate in a choir with eleven other Zambians that would travel the United States singing in malls, churches and schools. After passing the audition, Kachepa left on what he thought would be a two-year adventure that would provide him with an American education, a salary, money for his family and the chance to raise money to build schools in Zambia. "To have someone tell you that they could provide what you are missing, you think it is a gift from God," Kachepa said about the opportunity.

Kachepa's choir succeeded several previous choirs of Zambian students, who were promised the same thing. Unfortunately, he did not have the chance to talk to previous participants before coming to the U.S.

Trafficking . . . can be forced labor in a Chinese buffet restaurant or strip mall in your neighborhood. It is not your stereotype of sex labor.

His American dream soon turned into a nightmare as he found himself having little sleep, no money, close scrutiny, daily threats and the fear of returning to Zambia in disgrace. Kachepa had become a victim of human trafficking. "The threats were the biggest thing. In returning back they would tell your family and they would say you had no respect and respect is a big thing in Zambia," Kachepa said. "It was hard to ask anything. It came to the point where if you asked anything, they said you would be sent back." Deportation would have been viewed as a sign that a choir member had been disrespectful to their American elders; any choir member who had been deported would have been viewed as an outcast in Zambia.

The United States government estimates that between 14,500 and 17,500 people are trafficked into the United States each year, with 800,000 being trafficked worldwide each year. A study released, this year [2006], by the U.S. Department of Justice pinpoints the East Asia/Pacific region as being the largest source of individuals who are trafficked into the United States.

A breakdown provided by the nonprofit advocacy group Free the Slaves, states that 46-percent of victims are forced to work in prostitution, 27-percent are in domestic servitude, 10-percent work in agriculture, five percent work in factories, and the remaining 12-percent work in miscellaneous categories, including food service and consumer goods.

"Trafficking is a hidden phenomenon," said Martha Newton, director of the Office of Refugee Resettlement in the U.S. Department of Health and Human Services. "It can be forced labor in a Chinese buffet restaurant or strip mall in your neighborhood. It is not your stereotype of sex labor."

In the United States Kachepa would find himself being forced to work 18-hour days with little sleep. He would spend weeks at a time on tour forced into the back of a crowded van. The other singers—also from his village in Zambia—all found problems with their work situation. While on tour he had to clean his own clothes, set up and dismantle the equipment and live on little sleep. Very little free time was built into the choir's time on the road, with the only recreational activities being walking around the malls they performed in.

Constant Threats

Kachepa and his fellow choir members were threatened into not saying anything about their plight to the host families they lived with while on the road. Anything given to them by a host family had to be rejected. If a gift made it into a choir member's luggage, it was promptly seized by ministry officials.

Kachepa was constantly threatened with deportation if he did not live by ministry rules, which at one point included hand digging a swimming pool under the hot Texas sun.

"I questioned God so many times. Why would this be happening to me?" Kachepa said. "After everything I went through in Zambia, after things were supposed to be good, it turned out worse. Did God exist? How could I end up like this?"

Ministry officials regularly used scripture readings to reinforce their rules. The scriptures reinforced the ministry's desire to have the choir members respect them and their rules. Combined with the traditions from Zambia regarding respecting elders, Kachepa said he and the other choir members were conflicted about what they wanted to do. "We were hoping that God would liberate us from our situation."

After 18 months, the ministry called the police to start deportation against two choir members. After talking to the two choir members the police referred the case to federal immigration officials and the U.S. Department of Labor. The Labor Department forced the ministry to start paying the choir members and to give them educations. While Kachepa then started receiving a paycheck, he was forced to pay back most of it to the ministry in order to eat and sleep. By this point, several host families had been interviewed by the FBI as a part of the investigation into TTT and former Attorney General Janet Reno had been sent letters about the allegations.

The choir members called immigration officials and asked to be taken away from the ministry as conditions worsened. According to Kachepa, the ministry's founder, Keith Grimes, used the choir as a money making operation. In Kachepa's visa application to the federal government, he stated that Grimes said that if the choir members went home the choir employees (all of whom were members of Grimes' family) would lose their jobs. Though he was recognized by the federal government as being involved in human trafficking, Grimes couldn't be charged because the federal anti–human trafficking law had not yet taken effect.

Survivor

Following Grimes' death in 1999 his daughter, Barbara Grimes Martens, took control of the choir. Kachepa said Grimes Martens continued the same pattern. After the ministry was ultimately closed down, Grimes Martens moved away from Texas and has not granted interviews about the situation. A woman claiming to be Barbara Grimes Martens has posted on an internet message board refuting the allegations against TTT. Another Internet posting by Jonathan Elijah Grimes said that the allegations are false and that TTT built several schools in Zambia and provided home schooling for the choir members.

Documents filed with, and accepted by, the federal government as a part of Kachepa's petition to become a resident alien however stated that no schools were built in Zambia as a part of the choir coming to the United States. The documents state that the proof of no schools comes from previous choir members along with those on the ground in Zambia. As a part of the documents, Kachepa states that he learned from people connected with the first choir, that $250,000 had been generated by the first choir's recordings.

Kachepa would doubt his faith in God for putting him through the ordeal, which was supposed to rescue him from the depths of poverty.

The resulting federal investigation into TTT and Kachepa's ordeal resulted in almost $1 million in civil penalties being assessed against TTT.

Kachepa was granted a visa and certified human trafficking victims status by the U.S. Department of Homeland Security several years ago. With the help of a local Baptist church, he went to live with a local family active in the church. "I have observed Given coming into our family after being a victim" says Sandy Shepard, Kachepa's adoptive mother. "[I then saw] him going through depression and post traumatic stress. . . . As he spoke and shared his thoughts he released them and he forgave them. It was part of his ability to be a survivor."

Now 20, Kachepa is a student at Stephen F. Austin State University. He has been active in speaking about his ordeal and in lobbying the government for human trafficking policies. When not in class, Kachepa frequently travels the country to discuss the human trafficking issue.

In the years following his release from the ministry, Kachepa would doubt his faith in God for putting him through the ordeal, which was supposed to rescue him from the depths of poverty. He went through a depression and had to struggle to reconnect with the faith, which had been his inspiration in Zambia.

He was encouraged to go to church by his adoptive family and slowly regained his trust in God. He became active with a local youth ministry, which was tough since his English was not good at the time and he was struggling with the issues from his ordeal. Now he believes that he is back to where he was, spiritually, when he left Africa. He attends church regularly and goes to a weekly Bible study session on campus.

While Kachepa has turned his ordeal into activism, his fellow choir members chose different paths. Some returned to Zambia, while others in this country have primarily chosen to enter the workforce. Kachepa said that those in this country have not returned to their faith as he has chosen to do.

"God brought me along slowly and regained my trust," Kachepa said. "I pray a lot now. I will be watching CNN and see something and I will pray for it. I know God exists."

Women Traffickers Victimize Other Women

Claudia Núñez

Claudia Núñez is a reporter for the Spanish-language newspaper La Opinión.

"Gaviota" (not her real name) has six phones that don't stop ringing. Her booming business produces net profits of more than $50,000 a month. She has dozens of customers lining up for her in a datebook stretching three months ahead.

Gaviota is not exactly a college-educated professional, much less a businesswoman in a legal enterprise. But she has found "coyotaje" (illegal human trafficking) to be her best option of keeping the promise she tearfully made to her two children: "As long as they don't kill me, you won't live in poverty."

Women Are the New Coyotes

Gaviota is one of dozens of women along the southern border of the United States who are active participants and, often, the masterminds behind the world's third most lucrative illegal industry, after drugs and weapons: human trafficking.

Experts, authorities and the smugglers themselves agree that human trafficking networks are entering a new era, in which women have ceased to be the victims—smuggled across the border and often raped along the journey—and have become the ones that pull the strings in smuggling people ("goats," "chickens" or "furniture," as they call the undocumented).

"The old story of the man who runs the 'coyotaje' business is now just a myth. It's finally coming out that the big business of human trafficking is in female hands. As long as they make it known that they are women, they have lots of business all along the border," explains Marissa Ugarte, a psychologist, lecturer and founder of the Bilateral Safety Corridor Coalition of San Diego, California.

Many women have crossed the line that separates human trafficking from the trafficking of drugs, weapons and money.

In 2006, some 3,455 women were arrested for smuggling undocumented immigrants along the southern border, according to the Department of Homeland Security (DHS). So far in 2007, another 1,606 women have been caught.

Female coyotes tend to employ other women—most of them single mothers—to line up customers, arrange food and lodging for the undocumented, and participate in cross-border money laundering.

"A real 'coyote' organizes everything for you. From who and where to take the 'goats' across, and where they will stay on this side of the border, to who will deliver them to the door of the customer (the immigrant's family). The other ones who just take you across the river or through the desert— those bastards are just sleazebags and that's why we're eating their lunch," says Gaviota, whose smuggling network operates in Laredo, Texas, and transports migrants into the United States at border crossings or across the Rio Grande, depending on the customer's budget.

"The business is a real money-maker," says Ramón Rivera, a DHS spokesperson in Washington, D.C. "These women inspire confidence in the immigrants and when the authorities stop them and take them to court, they give them shorter sentences because they are mothers, daughters, because they are women. But when they get out, they go right back to doing the same thing, or worse—they start going into other areas."

Many women have crossed the line that separates human trafficking from the trafficking of drugs, weapons and money.

"I took my first 'chickens' across when I was nine years old, and when I grew up I started moving drugs across the border. My mother taught us the business and made us tough. She hated poverty. For her, power was everything," says Cristal, daughter of the notorious drug smuggler Rosa Emma Carvajal Ontiveros, "La Güera Polvos," or "the Blonde Powder Woman." Carvajal Ontiveros was shot to death on October 6, [2007] apparently by a hit squad, in Chihuahua's border zone with New Mexico, according to her family.

Just like their male colleagues, female coyotes put their lives at risk.

Corruption and Bribes Keep Traffic Moving

And like their male counterparts, female coyotes engage in extortion and bribery—of both Mexican and American authorities—which are prerequisites for setting up and maintaining human trafficking rings.

"In this business, everybody gets a share. The ministries, the Border Patrol and the narcos. You have to keep them happy so they let you do your job. Here, no money means no business," says Adamaris, a young woman in El Paso, Tex. As she tells it, her children's hunger drove her to turn her home into a "safe house" where more than 500 undocumented migrants have passed through in less than a year.

In addition to bribing federal agents, the women coyotes must also fill so-called "quotas"—monthly payments ranging from $5,000 to $15,000—demanded by members of the major drug smuggling cartels, in order to be allowed to operate.

"Nobody shows their face. You pay middlemen, but you know full well who the money is going to," says Adamaris.

According to the women *La Opinión* interviewed—all U.S. citizens except Adamaris—many female coyotes smuggle migrants through the border crossings, rather than the mountains or the desert.

"It costs more but it's safer. That's why they come to us. We don't mess around with walking for three lousy days in the desert, but you gotta have balls to take people across the border," says Margarita, who limits herself to smuggling women and children through California border crossings.

Female coyotes say they run these risks to avoid poverty and for the love of their children.

Margarita is motivated by economics—but in her case it isn't a fear of poverty, but her passion for "the good life." With her Coach brand sneakers and Dolce & Gabbana sunglasses, Margarita goes to the Mexican side of the border every weekend, looking for customers who will pay the tab for her luxurious lifestyle.

Penalties in the United States for human trafficking can be as light as one year in prison or two or three years on probation, as well as confiscation of the vehicle used to transport the immigrants. In the worst case scenario, those convicted of conspiring to transport and house undocumented immigrants get a maximum sentence of 10 years in prison and a fine of up to $250,000, or both.

This is why coyotes charge so much for their services: between $2,000 and $5,000 per person. They know that in every illegal crossing, there is the danger of making a mistake that could land them in prison for a long time.

Cases like that of Karla Patricia Chávez of Honduras, leader of the gang responsible for the deaths of 19 undocumented immigrants in a trailer in Victoria, Tex. in May 2003, have made a deep impression on Gaviota. "I knew that bitch. Texas is our turf, and we all know the 'little shops' (businesses).

That bitch didn't wise up, and she got found out. In this business, if you miss one little detail, they kill you or lock you up, and they take your whole crew down with you," says Gaviota, who keeps the names of her customers and employees under tight wraps.

The Real Forces Driving These Women

Female coyotes say they run these risks to avoid poverty and for the love of their children.

"We all got into this business out of necessity. Some of us are single mothers, and others have husbands in jail. The fact of the matter is that we're all on our own. What bastards are gonna blame us for what we do? Who wouldn't do the same thing if the miserable pay you get in a factory couldn't be stretched far enough to feed your kids, and you find you can get twice the money for just giving a drink or taking care of a goddamn 'chicken' (an undocumented migrant)? Anybody who blames us has never seen their kids cry out of hunger," affirms Esperanza, who smuggles undocumented migrants, money and narcotics in the Nogales, Arizona region.

Her taste for drugs, or perhaps her hard life, have prematurely wrinkled her skin. Esperanza, who is about 40, looks 60 years old.

But others say drugs and a lust for power are the real forces that drive women to enter the U.S.-Mexico trafficking business.

Nearly 90 percent of the women arrested at the Mexican border on smuggling charges are drug addicts, according to the organization Integral Family Development in Nogales.

"No matter how needy you might be, if you are an honest person, you're not going to get involved in illegal activities. Women like to brag about being more sensitive, more honest and protective (than men)—and that's not true with these women. Saying they're doing it for their children is just a pretext. It's really because they don't have enough money to feed their addiction," says Susana Padilla Gómez, director of the organization Integral Family Development on the border between Arizona and Sonora, Mexico.

Whether out of vice, power or hunger, it is clear that Gaviota, Cristal, Margarita, Adamaris and Esperanza—and the Blonde Powder Woman in her day—have won fame and fortune.

As Esperanza says, women's stories of smuggling must not remain untold, because, she says, "Getting laid by the coolest guy at the party isn't worth it if your gang doesn't know about it."

Organizations to Contact

The editors have compiled the following list of organizations concerned with the issues debated in this book. The descriptions are derived from materials provided by the organizations. All have publications or information available for interested readers. The list was compiled on the date of publication of the present volume; the information provided here may change. Be aware that many organizations take several weeks or longer to respond to inquiries, so allow as much time as possible.

Amnesty International (AI)
5 Penn Plaza, 14th Floor, New York, NY   10001
(212) 807-8400 • Fax: (212) 463-9193
E-mail: admin-us@aiusa.org
Web site: www.amnestyusa.org

AI is a worldwide movement of people who campaign for internationally recognized human rights. By providing articles, publications, pamphlets, and video media, AI seeks to educate the public about human rights violations and call people to action. AI publishes regular reports about worldwide human trafficking, including "End Human Trafficking" and "International Marriage Brokers."

Anti-Slavery International
Thomas Clarkson House, The Stableyard, Broomgrove Rd.
London   SW9 9TL
  United Kingdom
44 (0)20 7501 8920 • Fax: 44 (0)20 7738 4110
E-mail: info@antislavery.org
Web site: www.antislavery.org

Anti-Slavery International, founded in 1839, is the world's oldest international human rights organization and the only charity in the United Kingdom to work exclusively against slavery and related abuses. Along with partner organizations around the world, Anti-Slavery International focuses on debt bondage, forced labor, forced marriage, child slavery, human trafficking and descent-based slavery. In addition to an extensive library of publications available on its Web site, the organization also publishes the quarterly magazine the *Reporter.*

Coalition Against Trafficking in Women (CATW)
PO Box 7427, Jaf Station, New York, NY 10116
Fax: (212) 643-9896
E-mail: info@catwinternational.org
Web site: www.catwinternational.org

CATW is a nongovernmental organization that promotes women's human rights by working internationally to combat sexual exploitation in all its forms. Founded in 1988, CATW was the first international nongovernmental organization to focus on human trafficking, especially sex trafficking of women and girls. CATW's Web site contains information about trafficking in women all over the world, including their most recent publications, such as "Abolishing Prostitution: The Swedish Solution" and *The Links Between Prostitution and Sex Trafficking: A Briefing Handbook.*

Coalition to Abolish Slavery and Trafficking (CAST)
5042 Wilshire Blvd., #586, Los Angeles, CA 90036
(213) 365-1906 • Fax: (213) 365-5257
Web site: www.castla.org

CAST, a not-for-profit organization, was established in 1998 in the wake of the El Monte, CA, sweatshop case where 72 Thai garment workers were kept for eight years in slavery and debt bondage. CAST was created to provide intensive case management, comprehensive services, and advocacy to survivors healing from violence endured during slavery. In addition to an extensive library of videos about human trafficking, CAST publishes several resources annually, including *Disposable People: New Slavery in the Global Economy.*

End Child Prostitution, Child Pornography and Trafficking of Children for Sexual Purposes (ECPAT) International

328 Phayathai Rd., Rachathewi, Bangkok 10400
 Thailand
(662) 215-3388 • Fax: (662) 215-8272
E-mail: info@ecpat.net
Web site: www.ecpat.net

ECPAT International is a global network of organizations and individuals working together for the elimination of child prostitution, child pornography and the trafficking of children for sexual purposes. It seeks to encourage the world community to ensure that children everywhere enjoy their fundamental rights free and secure from all forms of commercial sexual exploitation. In addition to an annual report, ECPAT International publishes a number of resources, including "Commercial Sexual Exploitation of Children: FAQs" and *The Psychosocial Rehabilitation of Children Who Have Been Commercially Sexually Exploited.*

Free the Slaves

1320 Nineteenth St. NW, Suite 600, Washington, DC 20036
(202) 775-7480
E-mail: info@freetheslaves.net
Web site: www.freetheslaves.net

Free the Slaves, a nonprofit organization, liberates slaves around the world, helps them to rebuild their lives, and researches real world solutions to eradicate slavery. Free the Slaves was formed in response to Dr. Kevin Bales's groundbreaking book *Disposable People,* which introduced much of the world to modern-day slavery. In addition to providing a library of videos, books, and articles on human trafficking, the Free the Slaves Web site also houses an extensive list of the organization's original publications, including "Recommendations for Fighting Human Trafficking in the United States and Abroad" and "Ending Slavery: How We Free Today's Slaves."

Global Rights
1200 Eighteenth St. NW, Suite 602, Washington, DC   20036
(202) 822-4600 • Fax: (202) 822-4606
Web site: www.globalrights.org

Global Rights is a human rights advocacy group that partners with local activists to challenge injustice by promoting women's human rights and combating discrimination on the basis of race, ethnicity, or sexual orientation. With offices in countries around the world, Global Rights aims to help local activists create just societies through proven strategies for effecting change. Global Rights maintains an extensive collection of resources regarding human trafficking, including "Combating Human Trafficking in the Americas: A Guide to International Advocacy" and "Human Rights Standards for the Treatment of Trafficked Persons."

Human Rights Watch (HRW)
350 Fifth Ave., 34th Floor, New York, NY   10118-3299
(212) 290-4700 • Fax: (212) 736-1300
E-mail: hrwnyc@hrw.org
Web site: www.hrw.org

HRW is a nonprofit, nongovernmental human rights organization made up of more than 275 staff members around the globe. Established in 1978, HRW is known for its accurate fact-finding, impartial reporting, effective use of media, and targeted advocacy, often in partnership with local human rights groups. Each year, HRW publishes more than one hundred reports and briefings on human rights conditions in about eighty countries, including "The Island of Happiness: Exploitation of Migrant Workers on Saadiyat Island, Abu Dhabi" and "Workers in the Shadows: Abuse and Exploitation of Child Domestic Workers in Indonesia."

HumanTrafficking.org
PO Box 545, Dearborn, MI   48121
(313) 745-2379
Web site: www.humantrafficking.org

The purpose of this Web site is to bring government and non-governmental organizations (NGOs) in East Asia and the Pacific together to cooperate and learn from one another's experiences in their efforts to combat human trafficking. The Web site offers country-specific information, including national laws and action plans and descriptions of NGO activities worldwide. HumanTrafficking.org maintains an extensive library of publications on the subject of the sale and trade of humans.

Shared Hope International
PO Box 65337, Vancouver, WA   98665
1-866-437-5433
E-mail: savelives@sharedhope.org
Web site: www.sharedhope.org

Shared Hope International exists to rescue and restore women and children in crisis through education and public awareness. For almost a decade, Shared Hope International has partnered with local groups to help women and children enslaved in the sex trade by providing them with shelter, health care, education, and vocational training opportunities. In addition to an extensive library of interviews and press releases, Shared Hope International also offers free copies of the book, *From Congress to the Brothel: A Journey of Hope, Healing, and Restoration.*

World Health Organization (WHO)
Avenue Appia 20, Geneva 27   1211
   Switzerland
41 22 791-21-11 • Fax: 41 22 791-31-11
E-mail: info@who.int
Web site: www.who.int

WHO is the directing and coordinating authority for health within the United Nations system. It is responsible for providing leadership on global health matters, shaping the health research agenda, setting norms and standards, articulating evidence-based policy options, providing technical support to countries, and monitoring and assessing health trends. Several of its many investigative reports have focused on human trafficking, including "Second Global Consultation on Critical Issues in Human Trafficking."

Bibliography

Books

Beate Andrees and Patrick Belser, eds. *Forced Labor: Coercion and Exploitation in the Private Economy.* Boulder, CO: Lynne Rienner, 2009.

Claudia Aradau *Rethinking Trafficking in Women: Politics Out of Security.* New York: Palgrave Macmillan, 2008.

Alexis A. Aronowitz *Human Trafficking, Human Misery: The Global Trade in Human Beings.* Westport, CT: Praeger, 2009.

Kevin Bales and Ron Soodalter *The Slave Next Door: Human Trafficking and Slavery in America Today.* Berkeley and Los Angeles: University of California Press, 2009.

Kevin Bales and Zoe Trodd, eds. *To Plead Our Own Cause: Personal Stories by Today's Slaves.* Ithaca, NY: Cornell University Press, 2008.

David Batstone *Not for Sale: The Return of The Global Slave Trade—and How We Can Fight It.* New York: HarperSanFrancisco, 2007.

Karen Beeks and Delila Amir, eds. *Trafficking and the Global Sex Industry.* Lanham, MD: Lexington Books, 2006.

Sally Cameron
and Edward
Newman, eds.

*Trafficking in Humans: Social,
Cultural and Political Dimensions.*
New York: United Nations University
Press, 2008.

Steve Chalke

*Stop the Traffik: People Shouldn't Be
Bought and Sold.* Oxford: Lion, 2009.

Susan Dewey

*Hollow Bodies: Institutional Responses
to Sex Trafficking in Armenia, Bosnia,
and India.* Sterling, VA: Kumarian
Press, 2008.

Dessi Dimitrova,
ed.

*Marshaling Every Resource: State and
Local Responses to Human Trafficking.*
Princeton, NJ: Policy Research
Institute for the Region, 2007.

Theresa L. Flores

*The Sacred Bath: An American Teen's
Story of Modern Day Slavery.* Lincoln,
NE: iUniverse, 2007.

Anna Jonsson, ed.

*Human Trafficking and Human
Security.* New York: Routledge, 2009.

Maggy Lee, ed.

Human Trafficking. Portland, OR:
Willan, 2007.

Kimberly A.
McCabe

*The Trafficking of Persons: National
and International Responses.* New
York: Peter Lang, 2008.

Sarah Elizabeth
Mendelson

*Barracks and Brothels: Peacekeepers
and Human Trafficking in the
Balkans.* Washington, DC: Center for
Strategic and International Studies,
2005.

Tom Obokata — *Trafficking of Human Beings from a Human Rights Perspective: Towards a Holistic Approach.* Boston: Martinus Nijhoff, 2006.

Andrea Parrot and Nina Cummings — *Sexual Enslavement of Girls and Women Worldwide.* Westport, CT: Praeger, 2008.

Ernesto U. Savona and Sonia Stef, eds. — *Measuring Human Trafficking: Complexities and Pitfalls.* New York: Springer, 2007.

Silvia Scarpa — *Trafficking in Human Beings: Modern Slavery.* Oxford: Oxford University Press, 2008.

Clare Ribando Seelke and Alison Siskin — *Trafficking in People.* New York: Novinka Books, 2008.

Kara Siddharth — *Sex Trafficking: Inside the Business of Modern Slavery.* New York: Columbia University Press, 2009.

E. Benjamin Skinner — *A Crime So Monstrous: Face-to-Face with Modern-Day Slavery.* New York: Free Press, 2008.

Kimberley L. Thachuk, ed. — *Transnational Threats: Smuggling and Trafficking in Arms, Drugs, and Human Life.* Westport, CT: Praeger Security International, 2007.

Louisa Waugh — *Selling Olga: Stories of Human Trafficking and Resistance.* London: Weidenfeld and Nicolson, 2006.

Jeremy M. Wilson   *Human Trafficking in Ohio: Markets, Responses, and Considerations.* Santa Monica, CA: Rand, 2007.

Sheldon X. Zhang   *Smuggling and Trafficking in Human Beings: All Roads Lead to America.* Westport, CT: Praeger, 2007.

Periodicals

Joey Ager   "Freedom Songs," *Sojourners Magazine,* March 2009.

America   "Human Trafficking Victims Need More Help," December 3, 2007.

Bridget Anderson and Rutvica Andrijasevic   "Sex, Slaves and Citizens: The Politics of Anti-Trafficking," *Soundings,* Winter 2008.

S.M. Berg   "Pornography, Prostitution and Sex Trafficking: How Do You Tell the Difference?" *Off Our Backs,* July 2007.

Kevin Clarke   "Hidden in Plain Sight," *U.S. Catholic,* January 2009.

Liz Craft   "Making a Difference," *Times Educational Supplement,* October 24, 2008.

Michael Cory Davis   "Human Trafficking," *Hispanic,* September 2007.

Shannon Devine   "Poverty Fuels Trafficking to Japan," *Herizons,* Winter 2007.

Julie L. Drolet   "Trafficking and the Global Sex Industry," *International Social Work*, March 2009.

Economist   "Drawing Lines in a Dark Place," August 16, 2008.

Melissa Farley   "The New Abolitionists," *Ms.*, Spring 2008.

William Finnegan   "The Countertraffickers," *New Yorker*, March 5, 2008.

Barbara Glickstein   "The Tragedy of Human Trafficking," *American Journal of Nursing*, November 2008.

Viv Groskop   "Not for Sale," *New Statesman*, June 2, 2008.

Jeff Israely   "Where the Sun Shines Brightly," *Time*, July 14, 2008.

Andrew Jacobs   "Rural China's Hunger for Sons Fuels Traffic in Abducted Boys," *New York Times*, April 5, 2009.

Dawn Herzog Jewell   "Child Sex Tours," *Christianity Today*, January 2007.

Nicholas D. Kristof   "If This Isn't Slavery, What Is?" *New York Times*, January 4, 2009.

Mark P. Lagon   "Trafficking and Human Dignity," *Policy Review*, December 2008–January 2009.

T.K. Logan, Robert Walker, and Gretchen Hunt   "Understanding Human Trafficking in the United States," *Trauma, Violence and Abuse*, January 2009.

Susan Mohammad   "Prostitutes Are Okay, but Not Pimps," *Maclean's*, December 8, 2008.

Brendan O'Neill   "The Myth of Trafficking," *New Statesman*, March 31, 2008.

Caroline Preston   "From the Shadows," *Chronicle of Philanthropy*, December 11, 2008.

E. Benjamin Skinner   "People for Sale," *Utne Reader*, July–August 2008.

Emma Thompson   "Slavery in Our Times," *Newsweek*, March 17, 2008.

Jonathan Tran   "Sold into Slavery," *Christian Century*, November 27, 2007.

Christine Van Dusen   "Peonage in New Orleans," *Progressive*, August 2008.

Celia Williamson and Michael Prior   "Domestic Minor Sex Trafficking: A Network of Underground Players in the Midwest," *Journal of Child & Adolescent Trauma*, vol. 2, no. 1, 2009.

Index